W9-ABB-889

ATLA Monograph Series
edited by Dr. Kenneth E. Rowe

1. Ronald L. Grimes. *The Divine Imagination: William Blake's Major Prophetic Visions.* 1972.
2. George D. Kelsey. *Social Ethics among Southern Baptists, 1917–1969.* 1973.
3. Hilda Adam Kring. *The Harmonists: A Folk-Cultural Approach.* 1973.
4. J. Steven O'Malley. *Pilgrimage of Faith: The Legacy of the Otterbeins.* 1973.
5. Charles Edwin Jones. *Perfectionist Persuasion: The Holiness Movement and American Methodism, 1867–1936.* 1974.
6. Donald E. Byrne, Jr. *No Foot of Land: Folklore of American Methodist Itinerants.* 1975.
7. Milton C. Sernett. *Black Religion and American Evangelicalism: White Protestants, Plantation Missions, and the Flowering of Negro Christianity, 1787–1865.* 1975.
8. Eva Fleischner. *Judaism in German Christian Theology Since 1945: Christianity and Israel Considered in Terms of Mission.* 1975.
9. Walter James Lowe. *Mystery & the Unconscious: A Study in the Thought of Paul Ricoeur.* 1977.
10. Norris Magnuson. *Salvation in the Slums: Evangelical Social Work, 1865–1920.* 1977.
11. William Sherman Minor. *Creativity in Henry Nelson Wieman.* 1977.
12. Thomas Virgil Peterson. *Ham and Japheth: The Mythic World of Whites in the Antebellum South.* 1978.
13. Randall K. Burkett. *Garveyism as a Religious Movement: The Institutionalization of a Black Civil Religion.* 1978.
14. Roger G. Betsworth. *The Radical Movement of the 1960's.* 1980.
15. Alice Cowan Cochran. *Miners, Merchants, and Missionaries: The Roles of Missionaries and Pioneer Churches in the Colorado Gold Rush and Its Aftermath, 1858–1870.* 1980.
16. Irene Lawrence. *Linguistics and Theology: The Significance of Noam Chomsky for Theological Construction.* 1980.
17. Richard E. Williams. *Called and Chosen: The Story of Mother Rebecca Jackson and the Philadelphia Shakers.* 1981.

18. Arthur C. Repp, Sr. *Luther's Catechism Comes to America: Theological Effects on the Issues of the Small Catechism Prepared in or for America prior to 1850.* 1982.
19. Lewis V. Baldwin. *"Invisible" Strands in African Methodism.* 1983.
20. David W. Gill. *The Word of God in the Ethics of Jacques Ellul.* 1984.
21. Robert Booth Fowler. *Religion and Politics in America.* 1985.
22. Page Putnam Miller. *A Claim to New Roles.* 1985.
23. C. Howard Smith. *Scandinavian Hymnody from the Reformation to the Present.* 1987.
24. Bernard T. Adeney. *Just War, Political Realism, and Faith.* 1988.
25. Paul Wesley Chilcote. *John Wesley and the Women Preachers of Early Methodism.* 1991.
26. Samuel J. Rogal. *A General Introduction of Hymnody and Congregational Song.* 1991.
27. Howard A. Barnes. *Horace Bushnell and the Virtuous Republic.* 1991.
28. Sondra A. O'Neale. *Jupiter Hammon and the Biblical Beginnings of African-American Literature.* 1993.
29. Kathleen P. Deignan. *Christ Spirit: The Eschatology of Shaker Christianity.* 1992.
30. D. Elwood Dunn. *A History of the Episcopal Church in Liberia.* 1992.
31. Terrance L. Tiessen. *Irenaeus on the Salvation of the Unevangelized.* 1993.
32. James E. McGoldrick. *Baptist Successionism: A Crucial Question in Baptist History.* 1994.
33. Murray A. Rubinstein. *The Origins of the Anglo-American Missionary Enterprise in China, 1807–1840.* 1996.
34. Thomas M. Tanner. *What Ministers Know: A Qualitative Study of Pastors as Information Professionals.* 1994.
35. Jack A. Johnson-Hill. *I-Sight: The World of Rastafari: An Interpretive Sociological Account of Rastafarian Ethics.* 1995.
36. Richard James Severson. *Time, Death, and Eternity: Reflections on Augustine's "Confessions" in Light of Heidegger's "Being and Time."* 1995.
37. Robert F. Scholz. *Press toward the Mark: History of the United Lutheran Synod of New York and New England, 1830–1930.* 1995.
38. Sam Hamstra Jr. and Arie J. Griffioen. *Reformed Confessional-*

ism in Nineteenth-Century America: Essays on the Thought of John Williamson Nevin. 1996.

39. Robert A. Hecht. *An Unordinary Man: A Life of Father John La-Farge, S.J.* 1996.
40. Moses Moore. *Orishatukeh Faduma: Liberal Theology and Evangelical Pan-Africanism, 1857–1946.* 1996.
41. William Lawrence. *Sundays in New York: Pulpit Theology at the Crest of the Protestant Mainstream.* 1996.
42. Bruce M. Stephens. *The Prism of Time and Eternity: Images of Christ in American Protestant Thought from Jonathan Edwards to Horace Bushnell.* 1996.
43. Eleanor Bustin Mattes. *Myth for Moderns: Erwin Ramsdell Goodenough and Religious Studies in America, 1938–1955.* 1997.
44. Nathan D. Showalter. *The End of a Crusade: The Student Volunteer Movement for Foreign Missions and the Great War.* 1997.
45. Durrenda Nash Onolemhemhen and Kebede Gessesse. *The Black Jews of Ethiopia: The Last Exodus.* 1998.

The Black Jews of Ethiopia

The Last Exodus

Durrenda Nash Onolemhemhen
and
Kebede Gessesse

ATLA Monograph, No. 45

The Scarecrow Press, Inc.
Lanham, Md., & Lond⌐
1998

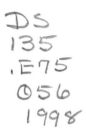
SCARECROW PRESS, INC.

Published in the United States of America
by Scarecrow Press, Inc.
4720 Boston Way
Lanham, Maryland 20706

British Library Cataloguing in Publication Information Available

Library of Congress Cataloging-in-Publication Data

Onolemhemhen, Durrenda Nash.
    The Black Jews of Ethiopia : the last exodus / Durrenda
Onolemhemhen and Kebede Gessesse.
       p. cm. (ATLA monograph ; no. 45)
    Includes bibliographical references and index.
    ISBN 0-8108-3414-6 (cloth)
    1. Jews—Ethiopia—History. 2. Jews, Ethiopian—Israel.
3. Israel—Ethnic relations. I. Gessesse, Kebede. II. Title.
III. Series: ATLA monograph series ; no. 45.
DS135.E5066   1998
963'.004924—dc21   97-46025
                                      CIP

ISBN 0-8108-3414-6 (cloth : alk. paper)

Durrenda Onolemhemhen
To my late father, Corbin Nash, and my mother, Alice

Kebede Gessesse
To my late father, Betwoded Gessesse Retta

Contents

List of Tables and Maps

Tables

Maps

Preface

I became fully aware of the Ethiopian Jews when I visited Israel for a conference in 1991. Although I had read newspaper reports about these people, my interest was heightened while in the country, so I took the opportunity to visit an absorption center in Jerusalem. Ever since the days of Jane Addams in Hull House, immigration and the assimilation of immigrants have held a special interest for social workers, and as a professor of social work myself I was interested in the human aspect of their immigration. I found the Ethiopian Jews to be beautiful in physical appearance, quiet yet friendly, and very much dedicated to their religious tradition.

When I returned to the United States, I decided to conduct a study of the Ethiopian Jews absorption process, as I realized that they are a unique group of world immigrants. With the assistance of Professor David Weiss, director of the Lautenberg Center for General and Tumor Immunology, Hebrew University Medical School, I went back to Israel in the summer of 1991.

Back again in the United States, I collaborated with Kebede Gessesse, a librarian at the University of Alabama. Mr. Gessesse is an Ethiopian originally from the province of Gondar, the indigenous home of the Ethiopian Jews, with useful insights into Ethiopian Jewry prior to its emigration.

While there have been other studies of Ethiopian Jews by Israeli and American scholars and journalists, we bring a new approach to the subject—the Afrocentric perspective. The Afrocentric perspective was introduced by an African American scholar, Dr. Molefi Asante, who coined the term. The Afrocentric perspective

emphasizes the customs of African culture and how it has pene-
trated the history, culture, and behavior of blacks around the
world (Schaefer 1993). This perspective determined our focus on
studying the Ethiopian immigrants through their own perceptions and convinced us that their interpretations of experiences
in Israel should form the focal point of the book. Furthermore, we
provide brief comparisons with other African people who have
migrated to the United States to live in its predominantly white
society.

Dr. Durrenda Onolemhemhen

Acknowledgments

Durrenda Onolemhemhen

To Professor David Weiss, director of the Lautenberg Center for General and Tumor Immunology, Hebrew University Medical School, I would like to express my deep gratitude. Professor Weiss's interest in and support of this book both initiated and sustained it through its completion. I would also like to thank his wife, Judy Weiss, for the hospitality extended to me during my field work in Israel.

I wish also to extend my gratitude to Danny Pins of the Jewish Agency; my field assistants, Maru Asmaru and Santaya Asmaru; my research assistant, Mason Voit; and Julie Faber of the Lautenberg Center. I also thank Professor Leon Weinberger of the Department of Religious Studies, University of Alabama, for his comments on the rough draft, and my colleague Allen Kaufman for his interest in the project. I most particularly thank Shafer Stollman, editor of the communications division of JAFI, for his permission to publish photographs and newsletter materials in the book.

To the Ethiopian participants who took time to discuss their lives with me, as well as government officials who paused during their work days to answer my questions, I give my sincere appreciation. I also wish to acknowledge the contributions to this book of my late colleague Dr. Amith Ben-David, University of Haifa, Faculty of Social Welfare and Health Studies.

To my mother, Alice Nash, I give special thanks for keeping my son Bukola safe and sound while I was conducting the field work in Israel for this book. My sons, George and Bukola Ojanuga, my daughter-in-law, Anna Luci, and my granddaughter, Gabby, served as an inspiration for my work. I thank my sister, Carmenletta, my brothers Corbin and Broderick, and my brother-in-law Mike for showing the kind of enthusiasm that helped to sustain me during the writing of the manuscript. Last but not least, I would like to thank my husband, Christopher, who is always loving by my side and supportive of my intellectual endeavors.

Kebede Gessesse

I would like to express my love and gratitude to my wife, Mantegbosh, for the great emotional support that she has given me over many years. Her faithful encouragement made my work a success. I also thank my children, Senait, Hirut, Daniel, Simret, Sosena, and Yoseph, and my adorable grandchildren, Amanuel and Bethlehem. They served, although without their realization or understanding, as my major inspiration for undertaking the writing of this book.

Series Editor's Foreword

Religion is as often responsible for ethnic character as the latter is responsible for faith. For state church adherents, a shared nationality, language, and homeland may overshadow religious beliefs and practices as the source of ethnicity. For religious dissenters, like the black Jews of Ethiopia, however, religious beliefs are their very reason for existence and survival.

After living in isolation from the Jewish community for more than 2,000 years, Africa's largest Jewish community left their mountain enclaves in Ethiopia for Israel beginning in the 1970s. Initially the desire for self-preservation was overriding in their new "homeland." Hostility bred fear and withdrawal again. The sense of peoplehood that the group brought with them to Israel was reinforced and in some cases awakened for the first time. Race plays a formative role in this process.

Recent studies of Ethiopian Jews undertaken by Israeli and American scholars and journalists have probed the process by which Ethiopian Jews inherited a sense of identity and common culture from their nation and religion but failed to take into account the Africanness of these converts to Judaism. This study by Onolemhemhen and Gessesse is the first to bring an Afrocentric perspective to bear upon this study.

We are pleased to be able to publish this ground breaking study in the ATLA Monograph series.

Kenneth E. Rowe
Series Editor
Drew University Library
Madison, New Jersey

Introduction

Over a 15-year period beginning in the mid-1970s, more than 40,000 Ethiopian Jews migrated from Africa to Israel. The return of the "Black Jews" to Israel is one of the unique phenomena of modern black history for two reasons: first, these Jews are the only group of Africans practicing Judaism, and second, they are the only group of Africans who have immigrated to a predominantly white society for religious reasons.

The religious history of Ethiopian Jews traces its beginning to more than 2,000 years ago, during the immigration of Jews from Egypt during Biblical times. Ethiopian Jews believe themselves to be the remnant of the lost tribe of Dan, one of the ten tribes of Israel captured by the Assyrians in 722 B.C. that vanished into history (Safran 1987). Others believe them to be the descendants of King Solomon and the Queen of Sheba (Kessler 1985). Although no one is really sure of their origin, people practicing a traditional form of Judaism lived in the mountains of Ethiopia isolated from the Jewish community at large for more than 2,000 years (Safran 1987). In their first encounter with Europeans, toward the end of the eighteenth century, Ethiopians were surprised to find that there were white Jews, because they had believed themselves to be the only Jewish people in the world.

Having suffered anti-Semitism in Ethiopia and always feeling as if they were strangers, the Jews of Ethiopia—or Beta Israel, as they called themselves—became anxious to leave Ethiopia for Jerusalem, their promised land. But unlike other Jewish groups it was difficult for the Ethiopians to gain recognition for returning to Israel. Finally, in 1973, Sephardic Chief Rabbi of Israel Ovadia

Yosef officially declared them bona fide members of the Jewish community and thus eligible to return to Israel as citizens under the Law of Return (Goldberg and Kirschenbaum 1989).

The Israeli government and the Jewish Agency, a quasigovernment agency in charge of immigration, attempted an airlift to Israel, but they met with opposition. The Ethiopian government had placed a general ban on emigration of its citizens. A few Jewish Ethiopians managed to escape to Israel, but massive security airlifts from refugee camps in the Sudan, where many Ethiopian Jews had fled, did not begin until the late 1970s. These initially carried about 8,000 Ethiopians to Israel from the Sudan. Operation Moses in 1984 brought another 8,000 Jews to Israel. By that time, Ethiopian immigration was in full swing. The flights were, however, abruptly halted when the press brought it to the public's attention and thus forced the Sudanese government, which is allied with the Arab nations, to stop all flights from its country to Israel. The flights did not resume again until the fall of the military government of President Mengistu Haile Mariam in 1991. President Haile Mariam initially had requested arms from Israel in exchange for the Ethiopian Jews, but the Israeli government denied this request. Instead, Jews around the world raised $35,000,000 to pay for the release of the Ethiopian Jews. In addition, the U.S. government promised Sudan a peaceful settlement of the conflict in Ethiopia with the rebel forces conditionally on their release.

Finally, in a dramatic rescue, Operation Solomon airlifted more than 14,000 Ethiopian Jews from Addis Ababa to Tel Aviv in May 1991. With the assistance of Israeli soldiers in plain clothes, the staff of the Jewish Agency, and other volunteer groups working with Ethiopian immigrants were flown without even a day's notice to Tel Aviv. They arrived in fewer than 33 hours in airplanes in whose seats had been removed so that they could allow as many passengers as possible on board. This remarkable rescue operation was widely covered by the international press.

Ethiopian Jews in Israel presently live in temporary housing such as hotels, caravans (mobile homes), or absorption centers. They are given an allowance by the Jewish Agency and in the first year are expected to learn to speak Hebrew at the ulpan, Hebrew language classes. The veteran Ethiopian immigrants are integrated into the Israeli community and are working, attending school, or serving in the military alongside other Jews of varying cultural background.

The purpose of this book is not to prove or disprove the Jewish origin of the Beta Israel but rather to look at its past in the hope of understanding its present situation in Israel. The story of these Jews is part of the saga of Israel, a country created in 1948 for the purpose of providing a refuge for oppressed people of the Jewish faith. Yet the uniqueness of the Ethiopians is that they were an unknown community for thousands of years—Lost Jews.

In part I, we lay the foundation of these people's past with an examination of pre-exodus Ethiopians. Social and cultural factors that fashioned their existence in Africa are described. In part II, we discuss the compelling political, social, psychological, and economic factors that motivated their exodus from Ethiopia. And in part III, we discuss the results of a study of Ethiopian Jews in Israel today and the factors that hinder and promote their absorption. Finally, we look at the factors that will determine their future in a new country.

BEAUTIFUL BLACK JEWS

Beautiful Black Jews,
Home in Israel, it's true.
Life again renewed,
Beautiful Black Jews.

—Durrenda Onolemhemhen
1992

Part I

The Ethiopian Jews and Their State

Chapter 1

Ethiopia: The Ancestral Home

For more than 2,000 years, the Black Jews lived in Ethiopia, a country situated on the Horn of Africa covering an area of 455,000 square miles. Ethiopia, whose capital is Addis Ababa, is bordered on the east by Djibouti and Somalia, on the south by Kenya, and on the west by the Sudan. On the northeast, it has 630 miles of coastline along the Red Sea, in which lie about 150 islands under Ethiopia's possession. The country is approximately 700 miles in length, northwest to southeast, and 640 miles in width, northeast to southwest. Its most southerly point is about 200 miles from the equator, while its northern extremity lies about the same distance from Mecca (see map 1). The population in 1990 was estimated to be 50 million, among the largest in Africa.

Throughout its long history, Ethiopia has always formed a bridge between Africa and Asia. "With its ancestry astride two continents and its position in the Horn of Africa," says Ullendorff, "Ethiopia has always occupied a favored place at the crossroad of civilization and a meeting point of many races" (Ullendorff 1960).

A mountainous country with great variations in altitude and climate, Ethiopia has at its center a high plateau divided into western and eastern parts. The western plateau rises from the Red Sea to the Kenyan border and has an average elevation of about 8,000 feet (2,400 meters) above sea level. It is characterized by steep gorges and abrupt escarpments that divide the highlands and make communication difficult among the regions of the country. The eastern plateau lies at a lower elevation and is less broken by valleys and gorges. It slopes gently eastward toward

3

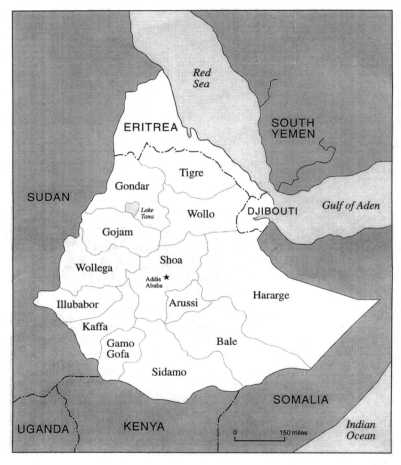

Map 1: Regional Map of Ethiopia

the Indian Ocean. Separating the western and eastern plateaus is the well-defined Great Rift Valley.

Ethiopia's climate is as varied as its geography. Most of the plateau region is temperate with a mean average of 60 to 68 degrees Fahrenheit. In contrast, the Red Sea coast is very hot. In fact, it is one of the hottest areas in the world. At the port of Massawa, in Eritrea, for example, temperatures higher than 120 degrees Fahrenheit are not unusual.

Ethiopia is one of the oldest kingdoms on earth. Unlike other African areas that have a history of colonial experience, the historic central territories of Ethiopia have only once in modern times, 1939–45, been ruled by a foreign power (by Italy under Mussolini during World War II) and the period was too brief to have any lasting effect on the centuries-old social and political order.

Ethiopia is a diverse country with complex ethnic and linguistic patterns. The two main ethnic groups are Hamitic and Semitic. Hamitic Ethiopians are sometimes called Cushitic, while the Semitic Ethiopians are known collectively as Amhara. Both are said to have entered the country from Arabia. Ethiopian Jews are classified as Semitic.

It is said that more than 75 different ethnic groups live in Ethiopia, though many of these groups are relatively small. The Ethiopian state today is largely a result of the historical role played by the Amhara and a related people, the Tigres. The Amhara, and the Tigres, are the country's dominant social and political groups, comprising one-third of the total population. The Amhara are commonly believed to be the descendants of ancient immigrants from southern Arabia, while the Tigres originated in the aboriginal Cushitic population of Ethiopia. The latter live in Eritrea and the province of Tigre, and the Amhara in the provinces of Begemdir (Gondar), Gojam, Wallo, and Shoa. Amhara colonies are also found throughout the country.

The people of the northern highlands are predominantly Amhara and Tigres, while those of the western grasslands and southeastern highlands are mainly Gallas or Oromos. In the southern part of the country the most important ethnic group is the Sidama, a collection of Cushitic peoples who once had strong kingdoms of their own before their incorporation into Ethiopia proper. The largest in number are the Galla. The Galla, although relative newcomers to the area (they are believed to have first entered Ethiopia about 400 years ago), today control much of the land in the south, central, and western parts of the country, and at about 40 percent of the population are the country's largest ethnic group.

Ethiopian people speak more than 100 indigenous languages. The Semitic people brought with them a South Arabian Semitic language which in Africa developed into *Ge'ez*, often called

"Ethiopic." Ge'ez ceased to be spoken in about the tenth or eleventh century, but it remained the ecclesiastical and literary language of Ethiopia. Three major living languages developed from Ge'ez: Tigrinya and Tigre, which are spoken in the north, and Amharic, which is spoken by 40 percent of the people south of the Tigrinya area and in the central part of the country. Tigrinya is the language most similiar to the original Ge'ez. Amharic, which has acquired substantial Hamitic accretions, is, however, the official language of the country.

In the south, four minor Semitic languages of Ethiopian type are evident: the first, Harari (*Adere*), is spoken in the city of Harar; the second is spoken in Gurage, south of Addis Ababa; the third (now extinct) was spoken in Gafat in the Abbai River area; and the fourth (which is disappearing) was spoken in Ankober, northeast of Addis Ababa.

English, the second language for education, is widely spoken by the intelligentsia and in official circles in modern Ethiopia.

Religion

The Ethiopian Orthodox Christian Church is the established church in Ethiopia, with the Abuna or patriarch as its head. It is a wealthy church, owning as much as 25 to 30 percent of the land, and popular; about 50 percent of the population follow Christianity. The provinces of Tigre, Shoa, Gojam, Begemdir, and parts of Wallo and Sidamo are mainly Christian; in those areas religion plays an important part in the life of the people.

Christianity came to Ethiopia in the fourth century, when the royal family converted to the new religion during the reign of King Ezana. By the eighth century, most Christian writings had been translated into Ge'ez by Syrian and Ethiopian monks. The Ethiopian Church has traditionally maintained ties with the Coptic Church in Egypt: the Archbishop of Ethiopia, under the authority of the Patriarch at Cairo, was required to be an Egyptian Copt. But the Ethiopian people never fully accepted this arrangement, and since 1950 that relationship has been cut off. Throughout the monarchical periods, the king or the emperor was also considered a titular leader of the Ethiopian church. Ethiopian Christianity places considerable emphasis on the Old Testament, and pious Christians often observe the Saturday Sabbath as well as the Sunday Lord's Day. Practices such as circumcision, food proscription, and rigorous fasting persist. Most Christian Ethiopians are extremely devout in their ritual observances.

Under Ethiopian law, there is freedom of religion, and Islam has been spreading into many provinces in the country, especially in areas where Christianity was not practiced. Islam is now practiced by roughly 20 to 30 percent of the population. However, for most traditional Tigres and Amhara, to be Ethiopian is to be Christian. The Christian Tigres and Amhara have been unwilling to adjust to the idea of a multireligious state.

Strong Judaic influences exist both in Ethiopian Christianity and in some of the traditional pagan religions. Judaism was practiced by the Agaw people in Dembia and Begemdir and Semien (Gondar) provinces, who are considered the Ethiopian Jewish ancestors of today's Ethiopian Jews. The Jewish population mainly use Ge'ez as their sacred language. They also have religious texts of their own besides the Old Testament.

Chapter 2

Lifestyle of the Jews in Ethiopia

Any study of the Ethiopian Jews must be set against the general context of what is known about the history and cultural development of the Ethiopian peoples who formed the first settlement in northern Ethiopia—that is, the ancient Ethiopian kingdom.

Calling themselves "Israel" or "Beta Israel," many Ethiopian Jews trace their origin from the Jews who accompanied Menelik, son of King Solomon and the Queen of Sheba, to Ethiopia between the third and fourth centuries. Other Ethiopian Jews claim that when the Hebrews left Egypt in Moses's time, some migrated south to Ethiopia; still others assert that they have descended from Jews who came later. The Amhara call them *Falasha,* a name derived from the Ethiopian word *fallasa,* "to emigrate." In the absence of reliable historical evidence, the origin and early history of the Ethiopian Jews remain a matter of speculation to Western scholars: "Whether they are ethnically Jews; whence and when they migrated to Ethiopia, or, on the other hand, whether they represent a part of the native Ethiopian population which was converted to Judaism, and if so, by whom—all of these problems still go unsolved" (Kaplan 1992).

The belief that the Beta Israel are the descendants of an indigenous people converted to Judaism stems largely from four facts: (1) most of them are indistinguishable in physical appearance from their fellow Ethiopians; (2) they do not know Hebrew, but speak the language of the people among whom they live; (3) Beta Israel culture, other than religion, is substantially the same as that of other Ethiopians; and (4) Ethiopian Jewish religious tradition incorporates pagan and Christian Jewish elements. Wolf Leslau's

9

investigation found that a few Falasha in the Semien area speak common Agaw dialects such as Quemantinya and Khamir. More-over, some old Falasha of Kwara, a district west of Lake Tana whence Quarrinya presumably was derived, still know an Agaw dialect they call Dembinya which presumably was derived from Dembya district just north of Lake Tana. Moreover, some of the Jewish festivals and fasts bear Agaw names, and Agaw is still used in many prayers and benedictions (Leslau 1950). These findings, however, do not detract from the significance of the dis-covery of Jews in Ethiopia: there are European Jews who are simi-lar in appearance to their fellow citizens, who do not speak Hebrew, and who share a culture with other groups. The German Jews, for example, can be as blond and blue-eyed as the non-Jewish German.

Despite the fact that they seem indistinguishable from other Ethiopians, it has been observed that the Ethiopian Jews devel-oped a strong sense of ethnic unity. And just like Jews dispersed throughout Europe, the Jewish population in Ethiopia lived scat-tered among the general population, mostly in Begemdir and Semien and Tigre provinces. Their number, estimated by the end of the seventeenth century to range from sixty to eighty thousand, had shrunk to between twenty and thirty thousand prior to their twentieth-century departure for Israel.

The Religious and Social Life of the Beta Israel

Of particular interest to this topic is the mutual dependence and clear similarities between Ethiopian Christianity and Ethiopian Judaism. The French scholar Maxime Rodinson agrees (Leslau 1950) that Ethiopian culture has been shaped far more by the imi-tation of the Old Testament than by direct Jewish influences. This view has also been supported by the German scholar and Ethio-picist August Dilmann, who contends (Leslau 1950) that many of Ethiopian Christians' biblical characteristics were not introduced in the Aksumite period, but only in the reign of the seventeenth-century emperor Zara Ya'eqob (1632–57) (Leslau l950).

It is the religious life of the Beta Israel that distinguishes them from other Ethiopians. Their beliefs and practices are similar in many ways to those of the Christians. The synagogue *(mesgid)*, like the church among Christians, is the center of religious life, and there is one in every large village. The synagogue is a simple structure, either circular or rectangular in shape, and often is indistinguishable in appearance from their dwellings. Sometimes the synagogue, like the Christian church, contains a sacred place set apart, known as the Holy of Holies, in which the Torah is kept.

Jewish priests (*kessem*), chosen from the general populace, perform the rites of the religion. These priests, like Ethiopian Christian priests, can marry but not divorce. Again like Christian priests, they wore turbans as a sign of their status. At one time, there was a monastic movement among the Jews, apparently derived from Christian examples, although since immigration, there are only a few monks left. Like Christian monks, the Jewish monks lived in seclusion in Ethiopia, could not marry, and seemed to be held in higher regard than priests by their community. The Jewish Scriptures are the basis of Ethiopian religious life and, like the Christian scriptures, are written in Ge'ez, an ancient Ethiopian script.

The Ethiopian Orthodox Church is absolutely faithful to the spirit and teachings prescribed in the Old Testament. As a result, numerous biblical customs have survived in the practices of Ethiopian Christians. For example, male babies are circumcised on the eighth day after birth. The Saturday Sabbath long held domain in Ethiopia and figures prominently in the ritual, liturgy, theological literature, and even politics of the church. Traditional Ethiopian dietary laws conform closely to those of the Old Testament, and the threefold division of churches in Ethiopia clearly replicates the architectural structure of the Temple in Jerusalem (Leslau 1950).

The presence of these and other biblical forms in the dominant Christian culture of Ethiopia raises a number of serious issues of direct relevance to the history of the Beta Israel.

Ethiopian Jewish worship, according to traditions, is focused on sacrifice on the altar, although animal sacrifice has been severely curtailed. Like Ethiopian Christianity and Islam, the Ethiopian Jewish religion involved feast and fast. There are weekly, monthly, lunar, and yearly festivals and fasts. The Sabbath is scrupulously observed in the Beta Israel custom: No work of any kind is permitted on this day.

Until recent times, the existence of monasticism among the

Beta Israel was just one of the many enigmatic elements in their history and culture. Research by scholars working with Beta Israel oral traditions has led to a better understanding of this phenomenon by placing it firmly in its correct historical context. According to Beta Israel tradition, the major catalyst for shaping their religious and social life was the arrival in their midst of a charismatic holy man, Abba Sabra in the fifteenth century. This monk is generally believed to be a Christian who had clashed with the reigning monarch and therefore sought refuge in the isolated region inhabited by the Jews. Instead of converting them, he joined them in their belief but brought with him the Christian institution of monasticism. His influence upon the religious life of the Ethiopian Jews is said to be very significant. According to Kaplan (1992), Abba Sabra irreversibly altered the basis of Beta Israel religious life.

The majority of Ethiopian Jewish texts reached the Beta Israel through the mediation of Ethiopian Christian sources. Perhaps the most striking example of this phenomenon is the best known of all Beta Israel texts, the "Te'ezaza Sanbat" (the Commandments of the Sabbath). This great work has long been considered the most original of Beta Israel compositions. Of its two sections, the second—the most important—is said to have been a skillfully edited and censored version of a Christian family. It has also been observed that the Beta Israel appear to have chosen works whose Christian versions already displayed a clear biblical Jewish tone. The deaths of major biblical figures, the celebration of the Sabbath, and the fate of the soul after death are all themes devoid of any exclusively Christian content. Thus, the Christian versions could be adapted for Beta Israel use without needing major rewriting. "On the basis of the present state of knowledge," Kaplan concludes, "it appears that Beta Israel literature offers strong support for the view that the early fifteenth century was a crucial period in the emergence of a distinctive Falasha culture" (Kaplan 1992, 75).

Land Tenure Rights

Land grants, or the confirmation of previous land use claims, were another essential part of the imperial policy of incorporation. The Beta Israel received new rights or had previous claims recognized at Kayla-Meda, Abwara, and other places in the vicinity of Gondar. One of the Gondar kings, Iyasu I (1682–1706), is reputed to have been the first emperor to issue the first kind of land grant proclamation by which the Beta Israel had been equally affected. The proclamation may have been part of an overall economic policy designed to rationalize the land system and regulate trade. By tradition, Iyasu is also said to have been the king who measured the land and established fixed boundaries. These efforts may have helped to resolve land disputes in a frontier area that for centuries had been characterized by virulent disagreements over land (Kaplan 1992, 114).

The Beta Israel Social Structure Prior to Immigration

The lifestyle of the Beta Israel in Ethiopia was a reflection of the lifestyle of Jews who lived during the first Temple period. Their yearly cycle reflected their daily living conditions and the special way in which they understand Judaism. The first day of each month was celebrated as a holiday, and the first day of the month of Nissan was considered the New Year, as written in the Book of Exodus. The Sabbath is the holiest day for the Ethiopian Jewish community. On Friday, all work ceased, and beginning at noon washing, bathing, and donning of Sabbath attire took place. Because it is forbidden to cook after sundown on this day, cooking was done during the day and fires were extinguished at sundown. Each woman prepared for her family a special baked dish known as *mosvait*, which means an offering for God or *birkhata* (blessing), and *tella*, a local drink similar to beer.

Generally the Falasha ate the same food as other Ethiopians, except that they did not eat raw meat, a popular food in the Ethiopian tradition. Exactly like the Christian Ethiopians, they did not eat animals that died natural deaths or those that had been bitten by a wild animal, like the hyena or lion.

Like other religious groups of Begemdir and Semien, the Ethiopian Jews allowed marriage only within their own group. Ethiopian Jewish girls were considered marriageable at age nine and boys at seventeen. Divorces were frequent, as among other people in Ethiopia. A child was given either a woman's Ethiopian name or a Hebrew name from the Bible, as with many Christian Ethiopians.

The Beta Israel had a strong tradition of circumcision. The circumcision practice was performed on the boys' foreskin and on the girls' genitals, a controversial Ethiopian practice. Circumcision normally took place eight days after the birth of the child. It was carried out in the menstrual hut, where the woman who gave birth sat surrounded by guests for the occasion. The high *kess* (priest) stood apart, chanting a blessing that recalls the covenant with Abraham and the forefathers and reciting the Ten Commandments.

The marriage customs of the Beta Israel were not different from the Christian Amhara-Tigris marriage customs. When a youth reached manhood, his parents searched for and chose a bride for him. The first contact was made between the fathers of the bride and the groom. If the bride's father found that the groom was acceptable and was from an acceptable family background, formal meetings would be held at which time the bride would receive gifts from the groom. The kind of gift depended on the status of bride's family; commonly, the bride's parents receive bulls in addition to other assortment of gifts. At the wedding ceremony, the marriage contract is signed before the kess and the witnesses. The bride is then brought from home to the hut where the groom and the guests await her. The kess preaches a sermon on marriage and blesses the couple that they may be fruitful, and the bride goes off with her husband to begin their new life together.

During the Gondar period of the fourteenth century, men supported their families by working as masons and carpenters building the city's new castles and churches while others became soldiers in the king's regiment. Some Beta Israelis in Gondar and its vicinity received grants of land and titles for their work as masons, carpenters, and soldiers. Their rewards of land and titles began to create new class divisions in the Beta Israeli society, with an elite that was upwardly mobile within the overall Ethiopian social structure, while the masses remained landless blacksmiths, potters, weavers, and tenant farmers (Quirin 1992, 99). Although they were incorporated to a great extent into the Ethio-

Perceived ambiguous identity leads to economic & social immobility for Beta Israel

pian political economy, the Beta Israel maintained their cultural and religious identity and held themselves aloof socially.

Beta Israel Villages

There is very little to distinguish a Jewish village from any other small mountainous villages—the only difference is an additional small tukul house called the "house of the curse," where Jewish women are confined during menstruation. Their synagogues are of similar structure as the Christian churches, except the former has a Star of David while the latter has the usual cross studded with ostrich eggs.

Waleqa was a typical village where a good many of the Ethiopian Jews used to live but only a few remain today. It is situated on Ethiopia's main north–south road in Gondar province. Another historically known place where the Jews once lived is Ambober, also in Gondar province (see map 2). Other than the evidence of the various crafts that typified Falasha life, Ambober is in many ways a typical Ethiopian village. Individual huts were surrounded by bushes and makeshift fences, each compound connected to others by rough paths. Ambober also had several mud-walled square or rectangular buildings with tin roofs, and there was no power source. At the center of the village stood the prayer house, a square building with stone walls and a metal roof, shaded by junipers and oleasters and surrounded by a rough fence. The changing names of the prayer house illustrate the shifting Beta Israel world. Originally it had been called the *mesgid*, the same name used for the mosque among Ethiopian Moslems. The term derives from a root meaning "to bow" and probably related originally to the Beta Israel (and Moslem) custom of bowing repeatedly upon entry to the prayer house and during certain prayers. But the building is also known as *selot bet*, literally "prayer house," by the Hebrew-speaking Jews. Those familiar with Jewish traditions abroad had begun, however, to refer to the prayer house with the Hebrew term *bet Knesset*.

The majority of Ethiopian Jews dwelt in small villages such as Ambober; only a few lived in the large cities. Their settlements were concentrated along Lake Tana, in the northwestern part of

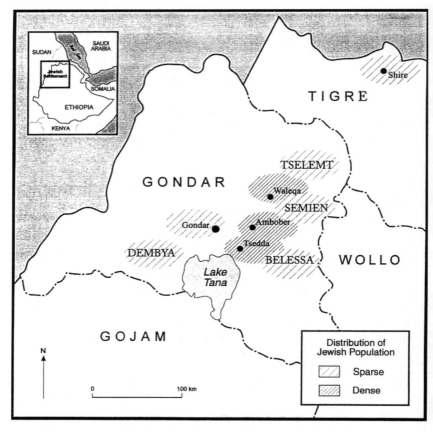

Map 2: Ethiopian Jewish Settlements

the country and in the high Semien Mountains. A number of families, usually related by blood ties, lived in the same village.

Occupations

As the main builders of castles and churches during the Gondar dynasty, the Beta Israel were rewarded or paid in goods and land, either in the form of grants or as royal recognition of their right to live in certain areas. It should be noted that these latter developments began to reverse the process by which the Beta Israel had been dispossessed of their land since the fifteenth century defeat by Yes'haq. As a result of their acquisition of land rights, some began to rise in status toward the middle stratum of Ethiopian society. They practiced agriculture as independent cultivators while still working as artisans in Gondar during that time. Once brought into the general Ethiopian institutional framework, the Falasha advanced through promotion and rewards. For those in the military, promotion to certain ranks was also possible (Quirin 1992).

On the basis of existing written and oral sources, it is impossible to determine with any certainty when the Beta Israel began to engage commercially in handicraft such as pottery, weaving, building, and most importantly blacksmithing. The major catalyst for their economic transformation seems to have been their loss of "re'est-rights" (land-holding right), a process that began in the fifteenth century during the reign of Yes'haq. Blacksmithing was an occupation that the Beta Israel had practiced since the fifteenth-century loss of land. During the Gondar era, they were known as "excellent smiths," making iron goods such as plows, sickles, lances, spears, and swords. However, there is controversy surrounding the fifteenth-century origins; according to some Beta Israel traditions they had been artisans since their alleged origins in ancient Israel (Quirin 1992, 97).

Quirin notes that the Beta Israel began to redefine their roles in Gondar—and within the Ethiopian social structure in general—by working as builders (masons and carpenters), weavers, and soldiers. The profession of soldier was particularly important to them because military ability was the single most important avenue of social mobility for non-Christians. Women diversified their occupations to become church decorators and paint-makers while they maintained their traditional role as potters.

Though not well documented in specific terms, it is presumed that the position of Jewish women was similar to that of Amhara women in Ethiopian society. Amhara women have the right to own and inherit property, initiate divorce, and recover from a marriage both the property they brought to it and a share of the wealth accumulated during their married life. It is presumed that Jewish women had similar rights. Jewish women, however, seem to have been subjected to severe limitations and restrictions as a result of their own cultural pattern. During their menses, they were separated from families in "huts of blood" or "huts of curse," and during childbirth their separation from males was more severe than that of women in Amhara society. And because of their occupation as potters, Jewish women were as despised and feared by the general Ethiopian public as Beta Israel blacksmiths. These were most often accused of having the "evil eye" or *buda*, because both professions required the use of fire.

The *Buda* Phenomenon

It is often asserted that Ethiopians called the Beta Israel *buda* and treated them with a mixture of fear and repugnance. A buda (evil eye) was considered to be both the spirit that possessed a person and the capability of causing the spirit to possess one. Several variations on the action of the buda were known from northwestern Ethiopia. At night, the buda was considered particularly dangerous; it was thought the buda could turn itself into a hyena and roam about digging up graves and devouring the cadavers. It was believed that if a hyena were harmed, the same injury would appear on the buda-person the next day. During the day, a buda could possess another person and cause him or her to turn into a hyena, donkey, cat, or other animals. The buda could also cause death or illness by using his or her evil eye to enter another person and drink the person's blood.

Although in northwestern Ethiopia mainly Jews were considered buda, the appellation of buda was (and is) not confined to the Beta Israel. At times, Christians, especially from the *debtera* class, were called buda. People from Gojam province (an Amhara settlement) in particular are often suspected of being buda—those accused may have been Beta Israel, Agaw, or Christian Amharas. People from any other ethnic groups—the Wayto, Muslims, Quemant, or any other—especially on first sight or encounter might be called buda. Also, any Ethiopian who performs manual crafts, particularly a metalworker, may be thought to be a carrier of the evil eye. Many Muslims and even some Beta Israel believe in the buda phenomenon, fearing its power as much as do the Christians. However, the buda appellation seems to have been rigidly attributed to the Beta Israel blacksmiths and potters.

And because the Falasha area is universally identified with black-smiths and potters in the Ethiopian social structure, this resulted in all Jews being identified as buda.

Education

Traditionally, the *kessem* taught only the Torah, and study and prayers took place close to the synagogue. They also served as teachers. Study was mandatory only for boys; girls were expected to receive their education at home from their mothers or grand-mothers.

Modern education among the Beta Israel did not begin until the 1950s. In 1956 the first group of boys was sent to Israel to learn the Hebrew language and other subjects. On completion, they returned to Ethiopia and began serving as Hebrew teachers in their villages. The first Jewish school was established in Addis Ababa earlier, around 1927, for the Jewish community in Ethiopia by Jacques Faitlovich, one of Joseph Halévy's pupils in Israel. However, Faitlovich's plans were halted by the Italian invasion in 1936–41 (Ethiopian Jewry 1986). He was forced to leave Ethiopia and abandon the school.

Prior to immigration, Jewish children had full access to enroll-ment in public and government schools. Some Jewish children had to walk many miles to get to the closest school, but this is not uncommon for Ethiopian children in rural communities.

In comparison to other Ethiopian groups, the levels of educa-tion of Beta Israel was generally low—a factor that would affect their lives after immigration to Israel.

Part II

The Exodus from Ethiopia

Chapter 3

Recognition and the Long Road Home

Many obstacles had to be overcome before the Beta Israel were legitimately acknowledged as Jewish and brought to Israel. There was very little mention of this lost tribe hidden away in northern Ethiopia until James Bruce (1730–1794), a Scottish explorer and active traveller in Africa, visited Ethiopia towards the end of the eighteenth century and wrote about his travels. The Alliance Israelite Universelle then sent Joseph Halévy (1827–1917), a French orientalist, to investigate the claim that Jewish people were living in Africa. When Halévy arrived in their villages, the Ethiopian Jews were surprised to learn that there were white Jews. After Halévy's return to Paris, a report about his experiences with the Beta Israel in Ethiopia was largely ignored, and no action was taken to help them.

The greatest assistance came from Jacques Faitlovich, a pupil of Joseph Halévy. Faitlovich first visited the Beta Israel in 1904 and returned to France after eighteen months with two Ethiopian Jewish youths. For Faitlovich, this was the beginning of a lifetime commitment to helping the Beta Israel gain recognition from the Jewish world community. He facilitated the training in Israel and Europe of Jonah Bogal, a young Ethiopian man. After completing his education, Bogal returned to Ethiopia to teach. Forty other Ethiopian youths were then taken to Israel to study. Faitlovich established a number of committees supporting Beta Israel around the world as well as a school in Ethiopia. He put the Beta Israel issue on the agenda of the Jewish world community by assisting Ethiopian Jews in sending letters for help worldwide. When the state of Israel was established in 1948, however, the Beta Israel problem was given low priority, as immigrants from Nazi Germany and the Arab nations poured into the new country. The Beta Israel were not officially recognized.

In the 1960s, the Ethiopian Jewish issue became a rallying point for Jewish activism in the United States. Leading this effort was Dr. Graenum Berger, a social worker who formed the American Association for Ethiopian Jews (AAEJ). This organization is still in existence today, working with the Ethiopian Jewish Immigrants in Israel (American Association of Ethiopian Jews 1991). The Jewish Agency, the Organization for Rehabilitation and Training (ORT), and other Jewish agencies established programs in Ethiopia for the Jewish population.

The efforts of many Diaspora Jews who firmly believed that the Beta Israel were Jewish, including the thousands of Beta Israel immigrants already in Israel, served as an encouragement to Chief Rabbi Ovadia Yosef, who officially declared the Beta Israel as Jewish in 1973, based on the claim that they were descended from the lost tribe of Dan (Waldman 1985). Twenty-five years after the creation of the Jewish state, Ethiopian Jews were finally given the right to return to Israel as automatic citizens. However, in 1973, Ethiopia was in political chaos. Emperor Haile Selassie was at the end of his reign. His political power had waned due to civil disturbances brought on by agrarian inequality and the government's insensitivity to the plight of the poor masses.

The agrarian crisis was a result of a small number of landed aristocrats and members of the royalty controlling most of the land in the southern part of the country, one of the most fertile parts. The Ethiopian feudal land tenure system was unproductive and could barely sustain the peasantry. Thus, when a drought occurred in 1972–1974 there was no food reserve, and over 200,000 people died of starvation:

> Numerous revolts against the government in the 1960s failed to spurn the aged Emperor into genuine social reforms, although some cosmetic changes were made such as the adoption of a constitution and the establishment of a parliament, which had virtually no decision-making power against the Emperor's highly centralized government. (Giles 1993, 339)

The Ethiopian Jews then were living in the midst of political problems as they had for centuries. In Gondar and Tigre provinces, the Ethiopian Jews had been unable to own land since the seventeenth century and lived in villages owned by absentee landlords who were paid a large percentage of the crops grown by the Beta Israel. The Jews also engaged in blacksmithing and became well known for the high quality of the farm implements and tools they made. Practicing a profession that used fire, however, aroused the superstitions of other groups who presumed that the Jews had a pact with the devil and were engaged in witchcraft (as discussed in chapter 2).

Feeling threatened by the hostilities of other groups, the Ethiopian Jews developed the survival strategy of isolation, living separate from Christians and Moslems in their own villages. The fear that their religious customs would be lost was another reason for their isolation. Their marginal status in Ethiopian society meant that they had virtually no input into the political decision-making process in the country, which was true of most minority groups.

One of the major concerns of the religious leaders (kessem) was the tremendous amount of pressure placed on the Jewish community to convert to Christianity. Conversion attempts by missionaries had been going on for years, and as a result many of the Beta Israel, in order to have access to modern education, jobs, and higher status in Ethiopian society, converted to Christianity. They maintained their links with the Jewish community through family members, however. Ethiopian Jews who were converted to Christianity are referred to as *Falas Maura*. Some of the Falas Maura were forced into conversion.

Non-Jewish contacts (other than with the Falas Maura) were discouraged by the kessem, and accidental interaction required cleansing of the affected Jews. For example, if a non-Jew ate at the home of a Beta Israel, the premises were considered contaminated and a ritual cleansing would be performed. Even European Jews, the first to make contact with the Ethiopian Jewish community, were not allowed to worship in the synagogue and freely interact in the village, as it was feared that they were not Jews and would contaminate the surroundings.

On a psychological level, despite their longevity in Ethiopia, the Beta Israel had never completely adopted a national identity, primarily due to their religious beliefs. They believed that their true home was Jerusalem and that they were displaced in Ethiopia. They were therefore psychologically bonded more to a country (Israel) they had never seen and a group of fellow worshipers whom for centuries they did not know existed than to Ethiopia and other Ethiopians.

The return to Israel was so much a part of their religious dogma, it is easy to see why in 1973, when the Ethiopians were officially recognized as Jews, they were willing to leave the country without a second thought. The news spread rapidly to the countryside, and there was a mass exodus of Ethiopian Jews to Addis Ababa for repatriation to Israel—only to find that the political climate in Ethiopia was unfavorable to their departure. Some Jews remained in the capital; however, most returned to the countryside.

In 1974, a year after their recognition, Emperor Haile Selassie was deposed by the military. The country was ripe for a Marxist revolution, and the military was the only organization strong enough to overthrow the emperor and his strong centralized government. Prior to the ousting of the emperor, the Ethiopian and Israeli governments had an excellent relationship. According to L. Rapaport,

> Ethiopia was . . . the linchpin of Israel's foreign policy in Africa. Israel built factories and established large farms . . . and engaged in joint enterprises in transportation, education, medicine, and geology. The Mossad and the Israeli defense forces advised the Ethiopian army and Imperial Ethiopian police as well. (1986, 50–51)

Rapaport (1986) further points out that Israel was reluctant to sever its ties with Ethiopia over the Beta Israel matter and the Ethiopian government was not in favor of the emigration of Ethiopian Jews to Israel.

With the demise of Haile Selassie, however, the period of cordiality between the two countries ended as a military Marxist-Leninist government was established in Addis Ababa. The country was run by a ruling council of military men called the *Dergue*, which clearly set Ethiopia on the path of socialism, as opposed to the democratic model the Israeli government favored. Within four years of the revolution Ethiopia was officially declared a socialist state (Giles 1993, 338).

The new government policy favored land tenure reform. They were determined to dismantle the feudal system of land ownership, which had created a large landless peasant class. Therefore, in 1975, all land was nationalized and redistributed to the disenfranchised. For the first time in centuries, the Ethiopian Jews became land owners. However, the military government's plan backfired as they had made no arrangements to enforce the land decree. As a consequence, Jews were brutally attacked and driven off their newly acquired lands by the former landlords and supporters of the deposed emperor's government. Atrocities were committed against the Jews:

> The reactionary forces of the Ethiopian Democratic Union (EDU), led by members of the emperor's family and other landlords, killed scores of Falasha and forced thousands from their homes in the late 1970s. . . . The EDU took over one Beta-Israel settlement and carried away the metal smiths and potters in chains to be sold in the slave trade. . . . village women were raped and mutilated. . . . men were castrated. (Rapaport 1986, 56)

In addition, the Ethiopian government placed a strict prohibition on emigration of citizens. This was particularly directed toward the Jews. In 1973, the Yom Kippur War began between Israel and Egypt, and Ethiopia, which was allied with the Arabs, officially terminated diplomatic relations with Israel.

In the villages, a number of Beta Israel felt they could wait no longer for repatriation to Israel and decided they would attempt to leave on their own through the Sudan. The Ethiopian province of Tigre was most accessible to the Sudan, and most of the earliest emigrants were from this area. The route from Tigre to the Sudan was rife with hazards. Ethiopian soldiers were stationed along the way, as well as gangs of bandits and thieves who preyed on bands of travelers. The journey, most of which had to be done by foot, was physically stressful with harsh conditions. Entire families attempted to escape using this route, and many people died before they could reach the Sudan; it was particularly hard on the elderly and the very young. Often, only one or two of the strongest family members were able to reach their destination. The emotional and psychological effects of the trauma experienced by the refugees would be felt long after their settlement in

Israel. An example of the trauma experienced during the journey to the Sudan is the story of the Dessie family (used courtesy of JAFI Communcation):

The Dessie family nightmare began in the spring of 1984, shortly before Operation Moses. A group of 70 Ethiopian Jews, including the Dessies and their seven children, set out on foot from the town of Azazo in the Gondar region of Ethiopia on an arduous month-long march to Sudan. The group was forced to travel by night and hide by day in order to avoid detection.

One night, the group reached a very steep incline. Menhale, who was only five at the time, was being carried on her father's back. One of the guides offered to carry Menhale so her tired father could get some relief. "Then suddenly, as we climbed the mountain in the dark, we realized she had fallen off the guide's back," recalled Rahel Imanget, the girl's aunt. "We searched for her for two days, but they told us she was dead. They made us continue, otherwise the entire group would be endangered. We cried all the way."

On September 30, 1984, Genetu and Dvora Dessie arrived in Israel with their remaining children. They settled in Migdal Ha'emek, and two more children were born there. But they never gave up on finding Menhale and were constantly questioning Jews arriving from Ethiopia. About six months ago, a new immigrant from Ethiopia told them he heard about a little girl found nine years ago by a Christian family in the village of Serteye and adopted by them. The Dessies turned to the Jewish Agency for help. The Jewish Agency chief emissary to Addis Ababa, Zimna Berhane, entered the picture. He began checking out various leads and succeeded in locating the family member in question. The agency then flew Genetu Dessie to Ethiopia in order to identify his daughter, who has a distinctive birthmark on her forehead.

When Genetu and Berhane arrived in Serteye, Menhale's adopted family, the Kebedes, told the pair that "one night, in the rain, we heard a knocking on our door. We thought at first it was an animal. She was almost naked, covered with filth and could not talk. She was close to death. We took care of her and when she recovered, we decided to adopt her." No one knows for how long Menhale wandered in the desert before she finally reached the Kebede home. Genetu and Berhane had succeeded in finding the Kebedes, but they still had not found Menhale. In a plot twist worthy of a Hollywood movie, Menhale had been kidnapped about a year before by a violent, drunken farmer who claimed she was his daughter and turned her into a virtual slave. Genetu, Berhane, and

Kebede spent two months running from village to village trying to find Menhale, but to no avail.

Disappointed and in poor health, Genetu returned to Israel to be hospitalized. But Berhane kept on in the search. He located the kidnapper, only to learn that his wife had left him, taking with her their children and Menhale. The wife gave Menhale to another Ethiopian family as a maid. Using local guides, and with the help of Kebede, Berhane was able to find this family in a village some 200 kilometers from Serteye. Menhale was brought to the Jewish Agency offices.

"Menhale has had a very hard life," Berhane said. "She's been hurt, humiliated, called an abandoned child. She told me about tear-filled nights and beatings. The family sent me a photograph and I showed it to her. She identified two of her sisters. This gave me the strength to continue. I knew then that she was truly the Dessies' daughter." Even so, in order to preclude any future legal complications, Menhale and the Dessies will be undergoing tissue-matching testing for absolute verification.

Menhale still faces a difficult adjustment both to her refound family and to life in Israel. An Amharic-speaking psychologist has been assigned to help her and the family cope with these new realities. But for her brothers and sisters, it was love at first sight. The youngest, five-year-old Hannah, almost at once took Menhale's hand. "I touch her and I feel she is my sister," said 19-year-old Ziva. "Praise G-d, and thanks to the Jewish Agency," said older brother Yair. "Menhale has been returned to us."

Not only did families like the Dessies who escaped from Ethiopia suffer, but the Beta Israel who remained in Ethiopia also experienced difficulties. Many young men were forcibly conscripted into the Ethiopian army. Jewish religious practices in Gondar province were restricted by the military government, and the Beta Israel were caught in the cross fire of rival political movements who were struggling for control of the country. While the Beta Israel were not the only group persecuted, unlike other groups their poor treatment was due to their religious rather than political affiliation.

On top of this political crisis came the drought of 1984, which caused further economic and political problems for the country. Thousands were dying, and massive amounts of foreign drought assistance from western nations was sent to help the starving masses. These political and economic crises in Ethiopia thus served as push factors for Jewish families to try to escape through the Sudan.

Operation Moses

As conditions worsened in the country, Tigre Jewish families were joined by Gondar Jewish families in attempting the long trek to the Sudan. Christian and Moslem Ethiopians also tried to escape the civil war in Eritrea province by trekking to the Sudan. The numbers of refugees were so large that camps on the Ethiopian-Sudan border were filled to capacity.

The refugee situation grew to crisis proportions as Ethiopians amassed in the camps. Initially, Jews were few in number in comparison to other groups such as the Eritrean and Tigrean Christians. The Jewish refugees were privileged in the sense that the Israeli government and Jews around the world were standing by to assist them, although they could not do so openly for political reasons.

Conditions in the camps were awful; poor sanitary conditions, disease, and shortage of food were common. Hostilities between refugee groups were widespread, and Jewish refugees were abused out of jealousy. When the non-Jewish refugees realized that the Beta Israel had the possibility of escaping from the Sudan to Israel, violence against Jews became frequent and sexual abuse of women common. In order to protect themselves, some of the women married at the camps, while other Jews concealed their Jewish identity for fear of persecution and arrest (Parfitt 1985). Despite the perils involved with escaping to the Sudan, members of the group retained hope that they would eventually be airlifted to Israel before the refugee camps took their final toll.

They were not alone. The Israeli government, volunteer agencies, and the U.S. government began a number of secret negotiations with the Sudanese government for their release and airlift to Israel. The main problem was the Sudan alliance to the Arab League, which forbid its members from having any diplomatic relations with the Israeli government. However, the Sudanese government was dependent on the United States for foreign aid. Sudan's economic condition was weak due to the Islamization Program, which brought back traditional customs of governmental rule that were ineffective and inefficient in the modern world, and because it had defaulted on loan payments and was unable to borrow money for government projects. Therefore, the U.S. government used the leverage of foreign aid to persuade the Sudanese government to allow the secret airlift of Ethiopian Jews from the refugee camps on the border. Although President Nimeiry feared the displeasure of fundamentalist Islamic critics as well as Arab allies if his assistance was discovered, a deal was finally struck when increased financial aid and assurances of secrecy were offered by the U.S. government. Another factor that influenced this decision, according to Ostrovsky and Hoy (1990), was when in "1979, Begin and Anwar Sadat of Egypt signed the Camp David agreement, Begin persuaded Sadat to talk Sudan President Jaafar Al-Nimeiry into allowing the Ethiopians to flow out of refugee camps in Sudan into Israel."

The agreement was that the Ethiopian Jewish refugees would be flown secretly from the Sudan to a intermediate country and then on to Tel Aviv. In addition to U.S. foreign aid, the Sudanese government was to be given all vehicles bought to carry the refugees to the departure area for the airlift. Four buses, four-wheel drives, and fuel were purchased for this purpose.

A Jewish-owned and Jewish-operated Belgium charter company, the Trans European Airways (TEA), was engaged to fly the refugees from Khartoum to Tel Aviv via Belgium (Parfitt 1985). The airlifts began on November 21, 1984. Assisting in the operation were Mossad undercover agents (most of them Ethiopians), Sudanese security officers, and members of the TEA company. Secrecy was the key word of the operation.

By the time the rescue had been arranged, the refugee camps were overflowing. At Un Raquba, the largest camp, there were more than 20,000 refugees—the majority of whom were Jews. The camp had originally been established in 1976 and was run by the Sudan Commission for Refugees in conjunction with the Sudan Council of Churches. Ethiopian Jews were dying there at a rate of eight per day because of deplorable camp conditions. In fact, in June 1984, within a 24-hour period, fifty Jews died. It was estimated that before the airlifts to Israel commenced, about 1,400 Ethiopian Jews died in this camp (Parfitt, 1985). Death among the camp refugees was an everyday occurrence. Ethiopian Jews who managed to reach the Sudan in reasonably good shape were, in a few months, reduced to skin and bones as a result of the poor treatment and poor running of the camps. Food, water, and medical care were insufficient for the vast numbers of refugees:

> In Um Raquba, Elizabeth Brobert, a Swedish nurse who arrived in May 1984, described her first sight of the Jewish refugees as, "lying all over the place." She says that there wasn't enough shelter. There wasn't enough food. We had very little medicine. . . . It was incredible how many died. (Gruber 1987, 150)

Jews around the world assisted the refugees with money brought to them by the Mossad, yet many Beta Israel died before they could reach Israel (Parfitt 1985). For over a year, Operation Moses continued, until the press exposed what was happening to the outside world and the airlifts were abruptly ended. During this period of time, 8,700 Ethiopian Jews were repatriated from the Sudan to Israel to join 8,000 other Beta Israel who had made their way to Israel by other means between 1977 and 1985 ("Coming home" 1991).

The "Other Operation Moses"

Victor Ostrovsky (1990), a former Mossad officer, gives an account of a little-known aspect of Operation Moses in his book *By Way of Deception*. He describes how the Mossad rescued Ethiopian Jews from the camps in the Sudan by establishing a tourist resort as a Mossad front on the Red Sea.

The tourist resort was registered in Khartoum as a project of a Belgian tourist company that wanted to promote water skiing in the Red Sea and sightseeing tours in the Sudan. A tiny water skiing club was bought out, and the site was constructed by Israeli and a few trusted Sudanese workers. Working in shifts, the workers constructed the club in about a month. At the same time, the Mossad constructed a makeshift airfield and a fully equipped communications center and stockpiled weapons.

In order to land the Hercules planes safely, Israeli intelligence located an area that was only partially covered by radar. This spot was near the Egypt–Sudan border. Aircraft flying at a low altitude could safely fly through the gap to the landing strip con-structed in the Sudan desert.

In March 1984, the resort opened, and the rescue of the Ethio-pian Jews began. The refugees were taken by truck to a meeting place in the desert. To get the trucks through their six-hour trip to the landing strip, roadblocks had to be avoided. High-altitude aircraft located the roadblocks and alerted the convoys. While there were a few minor incidents, for the most part the operation went smoothly. Convoy after convoy transported refugees to the airstrips where they were flown to Israel. However, some died en route. Ostrovsky and Hoy described the hardships:

> There were only supposed to be about 100 people (refugees) each time, but often twice as many would crowd into the trucks, weak, people jammed under a tarpaulin for a long, rough ride. Hundreds of Falasha, their bodies just too racked by hunger and disease, would die on this part of the trip, and hundreds more to Israel aboard the crowded Hercules aircraft but because they had been identified as Jews, they were taken, whenever possible, for proper burial in Israel. (Ostrovsky and Hoy 1990, 299)

The other Operation Moses ended at the same time as Opera-tion Moses due to leakage of information to the newspapers. In January 1985, the "resort" was abruptly closed, and the Israeli agents disappeared into the night.

Those Left Behind

The suspension of the airlifts left a thousand Jewish refugees stranded in the Sudanese refugee camps. Only four more plane-loads would have completed the mission.

In Ethiopia, 14,000 Beta Israel remained; some were too young to make a trek to the Sudan, while others did not have the oppor-tunity to escape from their villages. It was clear, judging from the large numbers of Beta Israel in Ethiopia, that the job of bringing them to Israel was only half done.

Life continued to prove difficult for those left behind in Ethio-pia as the political situation grew even worse. Lt. Col. Mengistu Haile Mariam, who had taken over the government from his mili-tary counterparts in 1977 after a bloody shootout at a *Dergue* meeting in Addis Ababa, was in trouble. The reforms instituted by his government had failed; most particularly, the state farms collapsed as a result of the drought of 1984–85. Other reforms that proved unworkable included the "villagization" policy, which combined smaller villages together for security and political reasons. Among the many villagers who objected to this plan were the Beta Israel (Giles 1993, 340).

The economy had grown so bad during the 1970s and 1980s that the government's primary means of economic support was foreign aid from the Soviet Union. Diplomatic ties with the United States had been severed.

Operation Sheba

The Ethiopian Jews stranded in the Sudan were in the most danger. Some attempted to return home, others were held by the Sudanese authorities, but the majority waited patiently in the camps to be rescued by the Israelis.

A diplomatic solution was achieved when U.S. pressure forced Sudanese leaders to agree to the airlift of the remaining refugees. The Sudanese were desperate for capital, yet they were unable to get loans due to nonpayment of past debts. Thus, when President Bush agreed to release $15 million in loans if the remaining Jews were freed, the Sudanese government eagerly agreed.

The responsibility for airlifting the Ethiopian Jews was given to the United States by the Sudanese leaders. On March 22, 1985, from a military base in Frankfurt, West Germany, nine C-130 transport planes were dispatched to the Sudanese for the rescue (Safran 1987). This operation was called Operation Sheba. On board were CIA agents, doctors, nurses, and a numbers of African American military men (Parfitt 1985).

As part of the agreement with the Sudanese government, the refugees were flown to various European cities and then sent on to Tel Aviv. Like Operation Moses, Operation Sheba was revealed to the public by a newspaper article. Unlike Operation Moses, however, there was no international reaction; the flights continued until the remaining Jewish refugees were flown out of the country.

Operation Solomon

Once Operation Sheba was ended, the airlift of Jewish refugees in Sudan was complete. However, thousands of Ethiopian Jews were still living in Ethiopia, in the midst of a civil war. Twenty-two thousand Beta Israel had settled in Addis Ababa close to the Israeli embassy, hoping to be taken to Israel. But the prospect of emigration appeared at times remote, and some families had waited for over a year. Living in Addis Ababa had been a difficult transition for Ethiopian Jews.

The Jews were basically rural people who had lived in isolation from the general populations for thousands of years and were unaccustomed to urban life. As a result, they fell prey to criminals, disease (including AIDS), and abuse generated by the prejudices and jealousy of other groups:

> The Jews in transit were the victims of recurrent assault, humiliation, insult, mugging, burglary, bullying of small children by teenagers and so on. Housing was poor as many of the Beta Israel families were only able to afford shacks and were living in tiny, cramped rooms, kitchens, or hallways next to open latrines. (Israel Yearbook 1991/2, 60)

As could be expected, the traditional community structure crumbled in the face of the stress of urban life. The Israel government responded to the needs of the Ethiopian Jews by providing them with much-needed services such as a medical clinic run on the embassy grounds and a school for the children. The school, which had 5,000 students, became the largest Jewish school in the world (The Jewish Agency Department of Immigration and Absorption 1992). Families were also given modest monthly stipends. Voluntary agencies such as the American Association of Ethiopian Jews and the Joint Distribution Committee organized social and medical services in Addis Ababa. And eventually an airlift was arranged to transport these remaining Jews to Israel.

The government of Ethiopian President Mengistu Haile Mariam had collapsed and was replaced by a military government. The Beta Israel community became a bargaining chip for the military government, which was threatened with the capture of Addis Ababa by rebel forces. Initially, the Ethiopian government requested arms in exchange for allowing the Jewish population to leave. Pressure from the U.S. government persuaded Israel not to grant this request. Instead, it was agreed that the Jewish population could leave if $35 million was paid to the military government. In addition, the United States promised that peace negotiations would take place between the government and rebel forces in London. Military leaders were eager for this settlement as they feared they would be overthrown by the rebel forces and the capital overrun if a settlement was not reached soon (*New York Times International* 1991).

Jewish individuals and groups raised and paid the $35 million bribe ("Coming home" 1991), and in May 1991, using giant C-130 transport planes and 747 jumbo jets, more than 14,000 Ethiopian Jews were airlifted 1,500 miles from Addis Ababa to Israel on 40 flights in just under 36 hours. The Israeli military led Operation Solomon with the assistance of American officials. "The complex logistics for the flights had been in place for weeks, but it took a letter from President Bush to the new Ethiopian leadership to prod officials to allow the Jews to leave all at once" ("Coming home" 1991, 36).

The day of deliverance began at sundown Friday, May 24, 1991, in Addis Ababa, where the first planeload of immigrants were to be flown out. The Ethiopians were informed of their departure only moments prior to takeoff. In an interview, one immigrant told how he threw the key to his apartment to his landlord and left all of his possessions in his haste to leave. Immigrants were allowed to take only a few personal belongings, hastily placed in small plastic bags (Fraser 1991). The idea was to carry as many people as the planes could hold, therefore all space had to be utilized, including that for luggage. All seats and interior walls were removed from the planes including the galley. Security measures were of paramount importance, and there was no time to adequately check the luggage. The rebel troops were close to Addis Ababa, and fighting had become frantic. No one knew how long it would be before the rebels reached the capital city, and by then it might be too late for the Beta Israel to escape. Time was of the essence.

At an empty compound close to the embassy, buses were waiting to transport the immigrants to the airfield. An advance party of 62 Amharic-speaking employees had been flown to Addis

Ababa several weeks earlier to drill the Beta Israel on the evacuation procedure as well as to issue transit documents to prospective immigrants (*Israel Yearbook* 1991/2). Ethiopian police escorted the buses to the waiting airfield where the Israeli air force was ready to airlift them to Israel. A surge of excitement mixed with apprehension pervaded the air, as family after family entered the aircraft. Life was terrible in Ethiopia, and war, famine, and death were everyday occurrences, but the familiar is always less frightening than the unknown. What would life be like in Jerusalem? This question must have been on the minds of most Ethiopian Jews as they departed Ethiopia on their way to Israel.

The arrival of the Ethiopians in Israel brought an end to a ten-year struggle. It also brought an end to the long road home and the beginning of a new life in a country much different from the one they left behind. It signified, as well, a reunification of black and white Jews and a recognition of religious affiliation between the Beta Israel and Jewish people of the Diaspora. Finally, Operation Solomon was the first time in history that people from Africa were transported to another country, not to make them slaves but to make them free.

Chapter 4

Home at Last

The Beta Israel, as they disembarked into the arms of relatives, Jewish officials, and others, appeared to be in a state of semi-hypnosis. Only hours before they were waking up to a typical morning in Addis Ababa and they were suddenly told that this was the day! Centuries of hoping and longing and praying among their people would be at an end today. Before they could grasp their situation they were airborne to Jerusalem, a dream come true. From Ethiopia to Israel, home, home at last!

When the Ethiopian Jews arrived in Israel, they were welcomed with open arms by the Israeli public, governmental and Jewish Agency personnel, soldiers, and volunteers (*Israel Yearbook* 1991/2). The drama of their escape from Ethiopia and the tremendous amount of effort the Israeli government and Jewish groups around the world had generated to get them there did not go unnoticed by the international press. Reporters and photojournalists by the score covered the story. When the planes began to arrive and family members were reunited, tears of joy flowed at the Lod airport. The tears were not those of the Beta Israel alone but also those of Israelis who had been active in the evacuation and Israelis who were just observers. A young Israeli soldier carrying a sick and aged Ethiopian woman down the stairs of the plane was asked if she was not too heavy. "No!" he said, "she is my sister."

Was this not history repeating itself with the saga of the Jewish people struggling for survival against all odds? The Jews this time were Black Jews from Africa, yet they were reminiscent of the Jews escaping from Nazi Germany, the Jews driven out of

Spain, and the Jews who had suffered persecution for centuries
because of their religion. Tears flowed not only for the Beta Israel
but for the Jewish people the world over.

The contrast between this experience and the experiences of
other African groups taken to predominantly white countries is
sharp. For example, Africans had been taken at gun point from
their homes, herded into vessels, as many as the hold of the ship
could take, and shipped to the Americas for sale into slavery. Unlike the Beta Israel, those Africans' humanity was snatched away,
stolen in the name of commerce and development; they ceased to
be human beings and became property. Characterized by the
slave traders and those who bought them as people without
souls, it was psychologically easier for them to oppress, subju-
gate, and enslave blacks because a man without a soul is not a
human at all. Dinnerstein, Nichols, and Reimers best describe the
views of white men who enslaved blacks:

> Africans (slaves) were not Christians, and whites gradually began
> to consider blacks, as they considered Africans, as beasts and were
> fascinated by the resemblance they saw between them and the
> chimpanzees discovered in the African explorations. White men
> also viewed blacks as lustful, sexual beings. These ideas eventually
> led to the ethnocentric conclusion that their darker pigmentation
> symbolized the innate inferiority of blacks. (1990, 68)

The Beta Israel, however, were brought to Israel not only as
human beings but as brothers in the name of Judaism, having the
full rights and citizenship accorded Israelis. This situation was
unlike that of African Americans, who had to fight for decades to
obtain the fundamental rights that the U.S. Constitution guaran-
teed white male landowners from the beginning.

The Ethiopian Jewish experience most closely resembles that of
the dark-skinned Yemenite Jews who suffered years of oppres-
sion and discrimination at the hands of their Moslem country-
men. Like the Beta Israel, the Yemenite Jews were restricted to
certain occupations such as weaving and silver and iron work.
They were excluded from the Yemen civil service and forced to
clean out animal and human excrement dropped down sanitation
channels (Weingarten 1992; Elazar 1989). They were also forbidden by the British to immigrate to what was then Palestine. Many

Yemenite Jews who were en route to Palestine prior to the ban were placed in camps along the way; some spent years there.

The first airlift of Yemenite Jews was in 1946. They were flown from camps in Hashed to Israel. As the Yemenites were evacuated, their place was taken by other Jewish refugees so that the camps were overflowing. The exodus of Jews was permitted because the Imam had died and his successor had an open-door policy and also because the newly created nation of Israel was obligated to take them (Lewis 1989).

According to Lewis, between 1949 and 1951, an airlift shuttle (called Operation on Wings of Eagles) flew the refugees to Israel. Forty-eight Yemenite Jews were evacuated to Israel, signifying the end of the Jewish population in that country (1989, 56–59).

Religion and the Ethiopian Immigrant

For more than 2,000 years, the Jewish community of Ethiopia struggled to maintain its religious identity despite persecution, discrimination, and continuous attempts by missionaries to convert them to Christianity. They managed to survive, clinging to the belief that one day they would return home to Jerusalem.

Called Falasha (strangers), they were denied many rights in Ethiopia, such as ownership of land and participation in the political process. A former civil servant in the Ethiopian Department of Agriculture tells how he concealed his Jewish identity in order to maintain his lucrative job in Addis Ababa.

The kessem (priests) were the backbone of the Ethiopian community as guardians of religious practices in Ethiopia, while isolation was the survival tactic adopted by the community when forces on the outside became too threatening. Immigration to Israel was a relief for them, ending years of persecution.

Despite their suffering, the Ethiopian Jewish community's identity as Jews is again under attack, not from gentiles but from the religious establishment of Orthodox Israeli Jews, who gained power when Israel was created to decide who is or is not a Jew. The kessem, who had held the community together in Ethiopia for centuries, reluctantly relinquished their power to the Israeli rabbinate, thus making themselves obsolete. They were no longer allowed to perform most of their religious functions such as marrying.

The attack on Ethiopian Jews within Israel took the form of recurring doubts as to the authenticity of the Ethiopians' claims to being Jewish, despite the ruling by the chief rabbinate that they were. When large groups of Ethiopians arrived in the Operation Moses rescue effort in the 1980s, it was decided that they were only Jews in terms of prayer service and burials; they were judged to be half-Jews in a sense and were required to undergo ritual immersion as part of a symbolic conversion to affirm their Judaism (Rapaport 1986). *VERY IMPORTANT*

Deeply hurt and insulted, the gentle-natured Ethiopians reacted with understandable rage, staging strikes in the absorption centers and demonstrations in Jerusalem. A compromise finally was reached, and the symbolic conversion ceremony was not required unless it was for marriage.

The religious issue arose again when the Ministry of the Interior adopted a policy of entering "Ethiopian," as opposed to "Jewish," on the identity cards of newly arrived Ethiopians. The justification was that some Ethiopians might have converted to Christianity and not really be Jewish. Again there was resistance by the Ethiopian community, which resulted in a demonstration in front of the prime minister's office.

The Jewishness of other immigrant groups had not been questioned in quite the same way, despite the possibilities of intermarriage before immigration. Gitelman points out that "the great majority of Soviet immigrants are not religious. . . . Very few had ever had formal Jewish education. None could belong to a Zionist organization in the Soviet Union" (1982, 69). In fact, 57 percent of Soviet Jewish men and 48 percent of Soviet Jewish women are married to non-Jews (Moskovitch 1990); yet there had been no request by the Chief Rabbinate for Soviet Jewish immigrants to undergo ritual conversion. Clearly, there was a double standard. Shapiro (1994) reports that the rabbinical court's power to determine the Jewishness of immigrants was struck down in 1994 by the Court of Justice. The petition was brought by the Religious Action Center (IRAC), a reform movement group. Subsequent to this ruling Ethiopian immigrants no longer had to be verified as Jewish by the rabbinical court, thus making it much easier to have "Jewish" placed on their identity cards and in the population census.

Klitah and the Ethiopian Jewish Family

In Africa the extended family system is the focal point of human survival, as this social institution nurtures the child, socializes the individual, and cares for the aged. The family serves as the mirror of one's position in society and as the major frame of reference in which an individual's identity is derived. Skinner (1973) best described the African extended family when he said, "In most African societies membership in a specific kin and descent group often determines a person's status and role, his rights, duties, and obligations" (1973, 247). More important, it serves as a safety net during times of difficulty, scarcity, and stress. In traditional African society it was the extended family system that provided the only means of social welfare for individuals in need as a formal system of social welfare and professional helpers did not exist.

The Ethiopian Jewish family before its immigration to Israel functioned in a fashion similar to other African groups. Family life centered around the village. The patriarchal family system was the norm among the Beta Israel, with the male heads of household making the major decisions for the family and providing economic support while women fulfilled the traditional roles of housekeeping and child rearing.

As in other African cultures, Ethiopian Jewish marriages were contracted through families and the choice of a mate was a decision of the group rather than the individual. "When a boy reaches adulthood—usually after the age of eighteen—his parents seek out a suitable girl, usually more than thirteen years old. . . . the two families celebrate three days before the wedding each in its respective village" (Waldman 1985).

The religious practices of Judaism were also a family activity. It was in the family that Jewish children were socialized into the religion, where the rituals, prayers, and etiquette were learned. The family also served to buttress the Ethiopian Jewish community against the outside world. Pressure to convert to Christianity was constant, and family reinforcement of religious values served as a deterrent to the forces of conversion. For centuries in Ethiopia the Beta Israel family structure, which adhered to religious practices, served as the stabilizing factor in an unstable environment.

The family was also the constant in the political uncertainty of

Ethiopia and in the face of prejudice and discrimination, a result of their minority status. In the face of the abuses of the dominant groups, Jewish families turned inward for emotional support and economic survival similar to other Jewish groups in the diaspora who have been confronted with anti-Semitism.

The critical question now is whether the Beta Israel families are Jewish or African families. In order to answer this question, it is necessary to identify those elements of Jewish life that are unique and separate from the culture in which they live. The most distinguishing factor is the practice of Judaism by family members and recognition of the family as such within the community where they reside. The Beta Israel family, while not initially recognized worldwide as Jewish, have always been identified as Jewish within Ethiopian society and always practiced a form of Judaism dating back to the first Temple period (Waldman 1985, 118). There can be no doubt that, within the confines of Ethiopia, Beta Israel families were Jewish families.

The African characteristics of the Beta Israel family structure cannot be disputed either. Unlike Jewish families in Europe and other parts of the world, Ethiopian families are extended as opposed to nuclear. In contrast with American Jewish family life, Ethiopian Jewish families are overwhelmingly dominated by male members of the family—a typical African family characteristic found in most parts of West and East Africa—whereas female members of the American Jewish family exert significant influence in family decision making. In some aspects, the Ethiopian Jewish family is more like the families of other Ethiopians than Euro-American Jewish families. Within the context of Israeli society, however, the Beta Israel family structure closely resembles the Presley Jewish communities of Asia and Africa, which are marked by strong extended families (Lewis 1989). This ambiguity of identity, where culture and religious practices both unite and separate Jewish families from the culture in which they live, is typical of Jewish families worldwide.

The lessening of family influences that were very strong in Ethiopia began as a result of the immigrants' attempts to reach Israel through the Sudan. Family separations occurred when members of a family, usually young adults, went to Sudan on their way to Israel, leaving other family members behind.

During the trek to the Sudan, the death of family members was a common occurrence, and some Ethiopian Jews reached Israel as the only surviving members of their family. Like Jewish survivors of the Holocaust, the family members who survived have had to bear the psychological scars of their bereavement for years, and in some cases suffer survivor's guilt manifested by suicidal behavior.

The need to adapt to a foreign culture alone, knowing that there was no return to Ethiopia, and the sorrow of losing family members through death or separation are the reasons behind many suicide attempts by early Beta Israel immigrants. A study by Ratzoni, Blumensohn, Apter, and Tyano (1991), at Beta Psychiatric Hospital, Petcha Tika, Israel, found that suicidal Ethiopian adolescents who went to Israel during Operation Moses in 1984–85 suffered cultural shock resulting in adjustment reactions, post-traumatic stress disorders, and depression. They point out that most of these youths had left their families behind in Ethiopia or had lost them during the trek to the Sudan. "Ethiopian families suffered from hunger and disease, were attacked by bandits and regular army troops, and many of them became victims of sexual and physical assaults" (1993, 293). However, according to these researchers most of the Ethiopian youths who came to Israel during this period have integrated into Israeli society, despite the difficulties, although some have developed serious psychiatric problems (Ratzoni, Blumensohn, Apter, and Tyano, 1991, 293).

A major change in the Ethiopian family structure has been the creation of single-parent families. In Israel about 20% of the olim families are female-headed households. This phenomenon was pointed out by Westheimer and Kaplan who estimate that, "among those who arrived in Operation Solomon, . . . somewhere between a third and a half were . . . one-parent families" (1992, 105).

The reasons for the creation of single-parent household are closely related to *aliyah* (immigration) and *klitah* (absorption). The death of a husband or wife as a result of attempts to reach Israel or the separation of couples as a result of different times of aliya is a contributory cause of single-parent homes. Klitah has resulted in changes in gender roles, and the elevation of the status of women has created conflicts resulting in divorce (Westheimer and Kaplan 1992).

A typical example of a female-headed household is subject 1, a 33-year-old Ethiopian female. When interviewed, she reported that she was an unemployed homemaker, with no formal education. She is the head of household because her husband was incarcerated 3 months before she left for Israel. She has three sons who accompanied her to Israel, ages 19, 15, and 12 years old.

At the time of the interview she was living with her children in an absorption center hotel in Jerusalem. She says that since her arrival in Israel 3 months ago she has three major problems: language, culture shock, and the environment. She says she has received no assistance with these problems other than ulpan language classes. She remains optimistic for the future, however, as she hopes by immigrating to Israel that her children will have an education and learn to fit into Israeli society. She wants to train as a merchant herself and get a good job. When asked if she had made the right decision about moving her family to Israel, she indicated that she wasn't sure if it was the best decision or not, as she had not lived in Israel long enough.

Family Reunification and the "Falas Maura"

Many Ethiopian Jewish families have been reunited as a result of Operation Moses, but not all members of Ethiopian Jewish families are eligible for repatriation under the Law of Return. The Falas Maura are a subgroup of Beta Israel who were converted to Christianity. Some were converted under duress and others did so voluntarily for political and/or economic gain (*Israel Yearbook* 1991/2). The exact number of Falas Maura is unknown, but estimates run as high as 20,000 in Addis Ababa alone. There has been considerable pressure on the government to allow this group to immigrate to Israel in view of the fact that they are relatives of Jews.

The Law of Return allows spouses and children the same rights and privileges as their Jewish relatives; however, this does not extend to extended family members such as grandparents, siblings, and cousins. While the doors of Israel were closed to the Falas Maura, they were not forgotten by their families in Israel. The movement for bringing them to Israel began to build after Operation Moses; however, there were mixed feelings among the

Beta Israel about their immigration. In fact, the community remains divided on the issue.

During Operation Moses, the Falas Maura converged on the Israeli embassy in Addis Ababa, requesting to be included in the airlift. However, the Ethiopian government objected to their repatriation on the grounds that they were Christians. Due to a lack of agreement between Israel and Ethiopia, they were excluded from the airlift (*Israel Yearbook* 1991/2).

In 1992 a series of hearings were held at the Israeli Knesset to determine if the Falas Maura should be allowed to immigrate to Israel. Israeli experts on Beta Israel and leaders of the Ethiopian community to Israel gave testimony to a committee of Israeli cabinet members and rabbis. On January 24 the committee announced its decision to allow only some of the Falas Maura to join family members who are already in Israel. Each case is to be judged on an individual basis according to which close relatives could be reunited with Ethiopians who clearly are Jewish and have already been brought here. It was decided that 100 Falas Maura who have children in Israel will be eligible for immigration immediately (Haberman 1993).

The Israeli government has been charged with racism for not allowing all Falas Maura to immigrate. The government denies this and says that their main concern is the increased economic burden the Falas Maura population would incur as a result of their absorption into Israeli society. The Ethiopian immigrants and their supporters point out, however, the double standard used for Soviet and Ethiopian Jewry. In the words of Michael Corinaldi, an Israeli lawyer, ''This is a double standard—one for the Soviet Jewry and one for the Ethiopian Jewry'' (*New York Times International* Jan. 25, 1993). Critics charge that Russian Jews seeking admission to Israel are seldom held to the same scrutiny as their Ethiopian counterparts.

The double standard used for immigration in Israel can be compared with the Haitian-Cuban immigrant policy of the United States. The 1966 Cuban Adjustment Act entitles people who flee the regime of Fidel Castro to special treatment in the United States, including a carte blanche status of political refugees and political asylum (Kirschten 1993). And the Refugee Act of 1980 permits the direct admission of persecuted people from their respective countries into the United States. However, this has not been the case for Haitian refugees, as they have been treated exceptionally harshly by the U.S. government under several Republican administrations.

Until quite recently the United States had a program of interdicting Haitian aliens before they entered U.S. territorial waters. The U.S. would then return Haitians to their home country before they could avail themselves of the provisions of the 1980 Refugee Act, which would entitle them to a hearing to determine their status as political refugees. Often the return to Haiti meant imprisonment or death for the refugee.

Pro-Haitian groups in the United States allege that the Department of Justice, the Immigration and Naturalization Service, and the immigration laws of the United States as they pertain to Haitians are racist in nature. According to the president of the International Rescue Committee, Cuban and Haitian refugees are treated "differently under United States immigration law [and this] points to a gross anomaly in this country's United States refugee policy" (DeVecchi 1994).

Although the situation of the Falas Maura differs from the Haitian refugee, the disparity of treatment when compared with Soviet Jews is similar. Whatever the case may be, total Ethiopian family unification cannot be accomplished without a satisfactory settlement of the Falas Maura question.

Ethiopian immigrant families, like African American families after slavery, are struggling to reunite after the trauma of their emigration experience.

Unlike in the African American experience, society is not intentionally destroying the Ethiopian family structure. Yet policies such as not allowing the immigration of Falas Maura to join family members in Israel, placing special requirements on the marriage of Ethiopian Jews, and settling families in cities far apart from one another may have similar if unintended effects.

Part III

Life in Israel

Chapter 5

The Study

This chapter reports the findings of an exploratory study using both quantitative and qualitative methodologies, conducted by Dr. Onolemhemhen in 1992. The social welfare research question to be answered was this: What can be done in the process of acculturation to maximize the Falasha Jews' successful integration into Israeli society?

A total of 72 Ethiopian immigrants were interviewed, 43 of whom were newcomer Ethiopians (*olim*) and 29 of whom were veterans (*vatikim*). For the purpose of this study, vatikim were defined as immigrants who had lived in Israel at least five years, whereas olim were immigrants of fewer than five years residence.

The olim were randomly selected from residents in two absorption centers: the Shalom Hotel, Jerusalem, and the Hulda caravan (mobile homes). A few respondents were from other caravans. The vatikim were living in Jerusalem and Tel Aviv. They were located in public areas, clubs, and schools and at their workplaces through word-of-mouth. Some of the respondents were nursing students at a Jerusalem hospital. A few were employees of the Jewish Agency and worked at the absorption centers.

Thirty-item questionnaires were administered personally to both vatikim and olim respondents. While many of the questions were identical, there were some items specifically designed to be answered by vatikim only.

The questionnaires were designed to determine their responses to the following items: (a) expectations for life in Israel, (b) problems encountered since immigration, (c) type and nature of assistance with problems, (d) interpersonal relationships with Israelis,

51

(e) experiences with racism and discrimination, (f) family status in Ethiopia, and (g) family status in Israel. The answers of olim and vatikim were compared.

In addition to the structured interviews with Ethiopians, informal interviews were held with government officials, Jewish Agency officials, and members of voluntary organizations working with Ethiopian Jews. The researcher also networked with members of the Ethiopian/Israeli communities attending social clubs, caravans, and public events where they congregate. This information was recorded in a field book.

Demographic characteristics of the sample and responses from the questionnaire were statistically tabulated and compared on the basis of olim versus vatikim families, using the SPSS and statpac statistical packages. Factors that facilitated and retarded adaptation were identified from an analysis of the responses on the questionnaires. Interview data were used to illustrate statistical responses, and secondary data were helpful in broadening the scope of the observations.

Findings

Demographic Characteristics

There were 43 olim interviewed, the majority of whom were married and male heads of household. Of the 29 vatikim interviewed, the majority were also males but heads of household were fewer as most of the vatikim were unmarried, young-adult children (see table 5.1). The mean age of vatikim was 29.7 years old and of olim was 38.2 years old. Nineteen percent of the sample were female heads of household.

The Ethiopian respondents had moderate-sized families; the mean number of children in olim families was 3.5, ranging in ages from 1 to 11 years old, and they were of primary school age, with a mean of 6.2 years old. The model age was 5 years old. Because most of the vatikim were single, there are no data for ages of children (see table 5.1).

Level of Education

When the olim were asked their highest level of education, almost half (46.5 percent) had no formal education at all, while 32.6

TABLE 5.1
Demographic Characteristics of Sample

Characteristics	Percentage	
	Olim ($\underline{n} = 43$)	Vatikim ($\underline{n} = 29$)
Gender		
Male	72.1	72.4
Female	27.9	27.6
Family Position		
Heads of Household	93.0	31.0
Female Heads of Household	19.0	
Adult Child	07.0	63.5
Other	00.0	03.5
Martial Status		
Married	72.2	31.0
Single	07.0	65.5
Widowed	03.5	
Separated	07.0	
Divorced	09.3	
No Response	01.0	
Mean Number of Children	03.5	
Mean Age of Children (Years)	06.2	

percent reported attending secondary school, and 4.7 percent had some university education. Table 5.2 shows that the vatikim group was better educated: 51.7 percent reported having completed secondary school (high school), while 24.1 percent had primary education. Those having no formal education accounted for only 17.2 percent of the vatikim, as opposed to 46.5 percent of the olim.

Occupations in Ethiopia

The immigrants most often were self-employed in Ethiopia. As shown in table 5.3, 32.6 percent of the olim reported their occupation as farmers, 11.6 percent as housewives, and 9.3 percent as craftsmen. Only 2.3 percent were businessmen, and there were no students among this group.

The responses of the vatikim were a reflection of their youth, as 58.6 percent reported themselves as students in Ethiopia, and

TABLE 5.2
Ethiopian Immigrants' Level of Education

Level	Percentage	
	Olim (n = 43)	Vatikim (n - 29)
No Formal Education	46.5	17.2
Primary School	07.0	24.1
Secondary School	32.6	51.7
University	04.7	
No Response	09.2	07.0
Total	100.0	100.0

TABLE 5.3
Occupations of Immigrants in Ethiopia

Occupation	Percentage	
	Olim (n = 43)	Vatikim (n = 29)
Farmer	32.6	10.3
Craftsman	09.3	00.0
Businessman	02.3	00.0
Housewife	11.6	06.9
Student	00.0	58.6
Military	00.0	06.4
Teacher	09.3	00.0
Other	27.9	00.0
No Response	07.0	17.8
Total	100.0	100.0

6.4 percent said they had served in the Ethiopian military. A little over 10 percent of the vatikim were farmers in Ethiopia, and five respondents did not answer the questions; perhaps they were so young when in Ethiopia that they could not remember (see table 5.3).

Occupations in Israel

While the majority of the population of Ethiopian Jewish immigrants were employed in Ethiopia, only three (7 percent) of the olim reported having a job in Israel. Table 5.4 shows that 81.4 percent of the olim were unemployed at the time of interview.

The vatikim reported themselves most often as students (37 percent), while 20.7 percent were soldiers. Other occupations included professional cooks (6.9 percent) and a craftsman; other types of work represented 17.3 percent of the sample (see table 5.4).

The data show that among olim there was almost total unemployment, whereas the veteran Ethiopians were working or preparing to work by attending school. Statistics from the Jewish Agency (1992) found that 20 percent of the olim from Operation Solomon were of working age and either participating in vocational training programs or employed.

The difference in the employment status of the vatikim and olim respondents may be accounted for in part by the differences in length of residency in Israel. The mean number of years for vatikim was 7.3 years, while for olim it was 9.4 months. It also should be noted that vatikim arrived in Israel at younger ages (17 years old), whereas the average age of arrival for olim was 22 years old. By arriving at a younger age, vatikim were better able to prepare themselves for careers in Israel.

Israel and Life Goals

While religion was the primary reason Ethiopians immigrated to Israel, their life goals were identified by asking what they

TABLE 5.4
Ethiopian Immigrants' Occupations in Israel

Occupation	Percentage	
	Olim (n = 43)	Vatikim (n = 29)
Student	00.0	37.9
Soldier	00.0	20.7
Farmer	00.0	06.9
Cook	00.0	06.9
Housewife	11.6	06.9
Craftsman	07.0	03.4
Other	00.0	17.3
Unemployed	81.4	00.0
Total	100.0	100.0

hoped to accomplish in Israel. When questioned about the goals they had set for themselves, 14 percent of the olim said they wanted an education, while 20.9 percent said they wanted a good job. Numerous other goals were given by 20.9 percent of the sample (see table 5.5).

Table 5.6 shows that education was the overwhelming response given (72.5 percent) when olim were asked what goals they had established for their children in Israel. Only 10 percent had no goals for their children, while 2.5 percent of the olim wanted their children to be "like other Israelis" and 2.5 percent gave other responses.

Vatkim also were asked what they wanted to accomplish in

TABLE 5.5
Ethiopian Immigrants' Goals in Israel

Item	Percentage	
	Olim ($n = 43$)	Vatikim ($n = 29$)
Education	14.0	44.8
Jobs	20.9	06.9
No goal	00.0	10.3
Getting to Israel	00.0	06.4
Other	20.9	20.8
No Response	44.2	10.8
Total	100.0	100.0

TABLE 5.6
Olim Goals for Children

Item	Percentage ($n = 43$)
Education	72.5
Become Israeli	02.5
No goals	10.0
Other	02.5
No response	12.5
Total	100.0

Israel. As shown in table 5.5, 44.8 percent said they wanted an education, 10.3 percent said they had no goals, 6.9 percent said they wanted good jobs, and 6.4 percent said that getting to Israel was a goal in itself. Of others, 20.8 percent cited numerous other goals.

When asked if they had reached or were in the process of reaching their goals, 34.5 percent said yes and 41.4 percent said no. Of the 29 vatikim interviewed, 10 felt they had not accomplished their goals.

The data indicate that the desires for better education and for jobs were strong "pull" factors for Ethiopian Jewish immigration. Many hoped for improved job opportunities for themselves and educational opportunities for their children. Although the majority of vatikim were students, there was a good deal of skepticism on their part as to whether they were progressing satisfactorily toward their goals. In some cases coming to Israel was a goal in itself, as Ethiopian Jews felt they were displaced in Africa.

Family Status since Immigration

The Ethiopian immigrants were asked the status of their families since arrival. "Better off," "the same," or "worse off" were the response categories offered. Table 5.7 shows that the majority (62.1 percent) of vatikim considered their families better off, whereas only 46.5 percent of the olim felt the same. Of the olim,

TABLE 5.7
Family Status in Israel

Status	Percentage	
	Olim (n = 43)	Vatikim (n = 29)
Better-off	46.5	62.1
The same	23.0	24.1
Worse off	16.3	06.9
No response	14.2	06.9
Total	100.0	100.0

16.3 percent believed their families were worse off, as opposed to 6.9 percent of the vatikim respondents.

The difference between vatikim and olim attitudes may be because olim are in the early stages of adjustment, living in temporary housing, whereas the vatikim are more firmly established, having survived the early problems of assimilation.

During the course of the interviews, both olim and vatikim respondents expressed the feeling that the economic situation of their families was tenuous. The olim felt that while their basic needs were taken care of, the allowance they received from the Jewish Agency ($25.00 per month) was inadequate. One of the vatik soldiers expressed anxiety over his parents, who were managing on a retirement pension at home, while he was posted at a military installation in another part of the country.

Most of the Ethiopian families found themselves at the bottom of the economic ladder. Unlike other immigrants (i.e., American Jews), they came with few if any assets, and middle-class Ethiopians often gave up substantial property to relocate in Israel. One middle-aged vatik head of household said he left behind a villa in Addis Ababa and two automobiles to immigrate to Israel. Another oleh related how he woke up one morning at 6:00 in Ethiopia and was in Tel Aviv by 10:00 that evening. When asked about his possessions, he said, "I just threw the key at the landlord and came with only the clothes on my back."

Other effects of immigration on the family are discussed at the end of the chapter.

Is There Discrimination against Ethiopian Immigrants?

One of the major differences between Ethiopian Jews and other immigrants is their skin color. The experience of other black people (e.g., African Americans) in predominantly white societies has been one of prejudice and discrimination exhibited by the dominant group. Ethiopian immigrants were asked about their experiences as blacks in Israel and how this had affected their lives.

The veteran Ethiopian Jews were asked if they had experienced discrimination in a number of settings, such as housing, schools, the military, shops, and social events. As seen in table 5.8, few

TABLE 5.8
Vatikim Opinions of Discrimination

Institution	Percentage ($n = 43$)		
	Yes	No	No Response
Schools	24.1	37.9	38.0
Military	20.7	34.5	44.8
Public accommodations	13.8	37.9	48.3
Social events	13.8	27.6	58.6
Housing	31.0	37.9	31.1
Other	10.3	13.8	75.9

Note: This question was not applicable to 5 of the respondents, as they had never lived in an absorption center.

immigrants reported overt discrimination. The data suggest that overt discrimination on the basis of skin color is not a serious problem in Israel; however, some form of covert discrimination does exist.

In the area of housing, for example, there have been problems. Occasionally, newspapers report Israeli tenants objecting to the presence of Ethiopian immigrant neighbors. A 1992 article in *The Jerusalem Post* ("Upper Afula" 1992, 3) reported that dozens of angry residents of a new neighborhood in Afula demonstrated against both the influx of immigrants from Ethiopia and low-income families. Renting to new immigrants and low-income families would turn the area into a slum, they charged. The residents maintained that their protest was not racist but based on economic considerations, yet protests are not held against Soviet immigrants who live there.

On November 11, 1993, the High Court of Justice, based on a petition filed by Yono Ephruin, gave the government 45 days to explain why it was preventing Ethiopian immigrants from settling in Beersheba, Dimona, Nazareth, Ofakim, and other towns (Gordon 1993). The absorption authorities denied racist motives on the part of their ministry and said the decision to restrict Ethiopians to certain parts of Israel was to promote integration by preventing the creation of ghettos.

It should be noted that, with the exception of an absorption caravan located on the outskirts of Jerusalem, there are few Ethiopian residents living in Jerusalem, the capital of Israel and a religious destination for people from all over the world. As has been the practice with earlier immigrant groups, most Ethiopian families have been placed by the Jewish Agency in development towns, smaller cities, and rural areas.

Although Ethiopian immigrants did not report many cases of discrimination, they do believe that there are prejudicial attitudes held by some Israelis toward them because of their African background. When asked if coming from Africa had any effect on their lives in Israel, 61.1 percent of the veterans answered in the affirmative. When asked how it affected them, 27.6 percent said they were perceived as being backward and uneducated, 24.1 percent say their black skin is problematic, and 10.3 percent gave other reasons, such as "We are treated better" or "I cannot reach my goals" (see table 5.9).

The data show that only a few respondents thought that society viewed their African background positively. Some Ethiopians (24.1 percent) thought their skin color was another obstacle to overcome in the process of assimilation.

Stereotypes held by some Israelis were exacerbated by the vast amount of publicity surrounding the airlift of Ethiopian Jews. The image portrayed by the international media was of villagers rescued from backwardness by their white brethren and plummeted into the modern world (Hull 1991). An Ethiopian soldier's remarks best illustrate this: "Israel is modern, so the Israelis treat you as if you came from the jungle; it upsets me. . . . I date Israeli girls sometimes, and people around hurt me by commenting regarding my origin. I don't let them know that I am hurt."

TABLE 5.9
Vatikim Perceptions of the Effects of Coming From Africa

Effect	Percentage ($n = 29$)
Perceived as backward	27.6
Black skin is a problem	24.1
Other effects	10.3
No response	38.0
Total	100.0

Another soldier complained that Ethiopian and Soviet soldiers were separated from others. He said, "I feel bad, because I like them (Israelis)." Ethiopian immigrants who were highly educated and had held professional jobs in Ethiopia were particularly resentful of stereotypical images. Newman (1985) believes that Israeli ethnocentrism is negative in two ways: first it creates stereotypes and generalizations about Ethiopians, and second, it prevents insights into Ethiopian culture that would promote understanding while reducing prejudice.

Zima (1987), in her observations of 42 Ethiopian boys who arrived on Operation Moses and were placed in a boarding school in a small development town in northern Israel, found that cultural differences in temperament between Israeli and Ethiopian students contributed to a racial clash. Ethiopian and Israeli students fought frequently during the first year. The Ethiopian boys were quiet, dignified, and sensitive, while the Israeli boys were louder and comparatively more grandiose. The Ethiopian boys fought by throwing stones, while the Israeli boys felt this was unfair and preferred fist-fighting.

These frequent clashes, Zima observed, resulted in the destruction of Ethiopian students' expectations of being accepted as equals in Israel and a consciousness of color where none existed before because Ethiopia was an all-black society never dominated by whites. As time passed, however, relationships between the two groups of students improved as budding friendship developed.

Despite these problems, Ethiopian immigrants interviewed during the study were grateful to be free of the hostilities that affected their lives in Ethiopia. A young male vatik said, "I have the freedom of having a good time at a disco; no one forbids me to do so. Jews could easily be killed in Ethiopia, so my mother did not let me go out much."

Ironically, while being a Jew was a problem in Ethiopia, coming from Africa proved to be problematic for Ethiopians in Israel. A measure of the level of acceptance of Ethiopians in Israel was an examination of their interactions with Israelis. When vatikim were asked if they had any non-Ethiopian friends, 72 percent answered in the affirmative; however, when asked how many, most vatikim reported that they had fewer than five non-Ethiopian friends. When probed further, it was found that most of the non-

Ethiopian friends were Sephardic Jews from Morocco, Yemen, and Iraq or immigrants from other African countries. Few mentioned Ashkenazic friends of European origin.

When vatikim were asked about the perceptions held by Israelis toward Ethiopians, 41.4 percent believed they were viewed favorably and 34.5 percent believed they were viewed negatively, while 13.8 percent believed that Israelis had no strong feelings either way (see table 5.10).

These findings were consistent with a survey of 3,400 young Ethiopian immigrants who came to Israel between 1984 and 1985 as part of Operation Moses. The majority (88 percent) of the Ethiopian immigrants felt that veteran Israelis viewed them positively; however, 41 percent of the immigrants met on a regular basis with other immigrants and only a small percentage had any regular contact with Israelis.

When the question was reversed, as seen in table 5.11, the majority of the respondents (51.7 percent) said they viewed Israelis in a favorable light and 13.8 percent had no strong feelings, while 3.4 percent viewed Israelis negatively.

The data show that vatik Ethiopians perceived themselves as having a slightly more favorable opinion of Israelis than Israelis have of them. As shown in table 5.10, olim held similar views to those of vatikim. A newcomer summed it up best when he said, "Everybody has different characters, so there are some people that help us as sisters and brothers, and some who do not."

TABLE 5.10
Ethiopian Immigrants' Views of the Perceptions Held by Israelis Toward Them

View	Percentage	
	Olim (n = 43)	Vatikim (n = 29)
Viewed favorably	34.9	41.4
Viewed negatively	09.3	34.5
No strong feelings	14.0	13.8
Other	04.6	00.0
No response	37.2	10.3
Total	100.0	100.0

TABLE 5.11
Vatikim Perceptions of Israelis

Perception	Percentage ($\underline{n}$ = 29)
Viewed favorably	51.7
Viewed negatively	03.4
No strong feelings	13.8
No response	31.1
Total	100.0

Ethiopian Immigrants' Relationships with Other Immigrant Groups

The questionnaire did not have any questions regarding Ethiopians' relationships with other immigrants, but informal interviews with Jewish Agency officials and Ethiopian immigrants gave interesting insights into this aspect of absorption. What happens when two groups of immigrants find themselves competing for scarce resources? How do different immigrant groups interact as they experience the problems of adjusting to a new life?

Soviet Jews

A Jewish Agency employee interviewed said that often Soviet immigrants objected to the presence of Ethiopians in Israel on the grounds that they "carry diseases" and are "primitive"; some Israelis suggest that Ethiopians have AIDS. Most certainly the health status of Ethiopian immigrants was affected by inadequate health facilities, drought, and famine in Ethiopia. Some Ethiopian immigrants arrived in poor health, a result of malaria, intestinal parasites, tuberculosis, syphilis, Hepatitis B, conditions associated with low-economic status, and a tropical climate. Some were underweight in comparison to the norm for Israelis (American Association of Ethiopian Jews 1991). Ethiopian olim, however, posed no threat to other immigrants, as within a week of arrival complete medical exams and any needed immunizations were given. According to a report of the American Association of Ethiopian Jews (1991), the seriously ill were sent to hospitals, and treatment was started for those who needed it. The fear of the Soviet immigrants that the Ethiopians have AIDS is also unfounded. The insular nature of the Ethiopian Jewish community protected it from interaction with other groups in Ethiopia; therefore, there have been few reported cases of HIV-positive Ethiopian olim. However, in 1995, Ethiopian immigrants drew worldwide attention when they rioted after discovering that blood donated by Ethiopians had been disposed of due to a fear of AIDS. The blood donor agencies explained that Ethiopians were believed to have high rates of AIDS; but they did not want to hurt the feelings of the donors by refusing their blood. However, the blood could have been tested. An incident such as this feeds stereotypes about Ethiopians and makes it more difficult for them to be accepted by other Israelis.

Soviet immigrants also complained that Ethiopians were given more in terms of material goods, without realizing that many items were donated specifically to Ethiopians who had fewer material possessions than other immigrant groups.

On August 26, 1991, the tension between Ethiopians and Soviet immigrants rose so high that a brawl erupted at the Jerusalem Diplomat Hotel where four people were injured. According to the Ethiopians, Soviet immigrants did not want to occupy the same elevator with them. The Ethiopian olim were told by the Soviets not to get on the elevator. If the Soviets were the first to enter, Ethiopians were forced to wait until the elevator returned empty. Understandably, the Ethiopian immigrants objected to this form of discrimination, and struggles over the elevators erupted into a free-for-all fist fight in the lobby of the hotel. The incident was reported by the media the following day. A month later, the Ethiopians were moved out of the Diplomat Hotel to absorption centers around the country.

South African Jews

During the era of apartheid, the South African government and Israel had close economic ties. In fact, the former South African president, F. W. de Klerk, visited Israel and promised that South Africa would remain a trustworthy friend to Israel. Immigration by South African Jews to Israel constitutes a significant number of immigrants to the country. In 1990, the Israeli Central Bureau of Statistics reported that 2.9 percent of immigrants that year were Jews from the Republic of South Africa.

Serious allegations were lodged against the Israeli government by a former agent that the Israeli had helped the Republic of South Africa build nuclear weapons during the apartheid era (Ostrovsky and Hoy 1990). However, this allegation was denied by the Israeli government, and there has been no substantial evidence to support the allegation. Yet, Israel's close ties with the then-repressive government of South Africa raise the question whether Ethiopian Jews would be treated fairly by South African Jews in Israel.

While there are no empirical data regarding the relationship between South African Jews and Ethiopian immigrants in Israel, information of this nature would be helpful in assisting with the absorption of both groups, considering the possibility that some South African Jews might have left the country in order to avoid the repressive apartheid South African government.

Israelis and the Sephardic Jews

Regarding Israeli and Ethiopian social interaction, it is helpful to look at the experiences of other groups who immigrated to Israel in similar circumstances. The Sephardic Jews have struggled to maintain identity and self-respect under tremendous pressures brought on by the controlling European elite (Ashkenazim). Absorption in this context meant Europeanization, and the Arabic-like culture of the Sephardic Jews was considered inferior.

Elazar (1989), in his book *The Other Jew*, tells of some experiences of dark-skinned Yemenite Jews who were airlifted to Israel in the 1950s. Newborns and young children were removed from their parents and sent off to live with Ashkenazic families who, it was believed, would help the children overcome their "backwardness." Thirty-five years later, in 1985, an investigation was held and apologies made, but the damage had been done: the children were lost to their parents forever.

Other examples cited by Elazar (1989) involved Sephardic children leaving school after the seventh grade to work as farm laborers and Iraqi Jews being forced to live in tents so that Romanian

Jewish immigrants could take over the permanent buildings. The assumption was that Jews from Arab lands were used to living in tents while immigrants from Europe were not.

The lessons learned from the experiences of Sephardic Jews must be applied to Ethiopian immigrants, so that the same mistakes are not repeated with the Ethiopians. The major lesson is that ethnocentrism among government officials and the Israeli community must not be tolerated, particularly among those administering absorption programs. Furthermore, policy decisions should not be based on the European norm; rather, immigrants should be allowed to reach an adjustment consistent with their cultural background, yet functional in terms of the society at large.

Chapter 6

The Vatikim Experience

What is life like for immigrants who arrived earlier and are no longer officially under the guardianship of the Jewish Agency? As described in an earlier section of this book, the vatikim population surveyed had been in Israel for an average of 7.345 years. The mode was 7 years, with a standard deviation of 2.327 years. The mean age of the respondents was 29.7 years, with a mode of 21 years old. The mean age of arrival was 22 years.

The majority of the vatikim were working in the military or were housewives or students. For the most part, Ethiopian vatikim were employed as laborers in low-skilled jobs such as cooks, daily workers, and clerks. Students in the sample were training for skilled jobs such as nurses and mechanics. A number of the vatikim with strong educational backgrounds were employed by the Jewish Agency as translators.

Most of the vatikim interviewed were doing fairly well. They had completed primary school, had salaried employment, and attended synagogue regularly, etc. Yet few reported owning property in Israel, and they were at the bottom of the economic scale when compared with other Israelis.

When asked what they missed most about Ethiopia, they most frequently said their birthplace (37.9 pecent), family members (17.2 percent), and friends (6.9 percent); other items accounted for 17.2 percent of the responses.

When asked the greatest problem of living in Israel, the majority said the language. When asked the best aspect of living in Israel, the answer most often given was "living in my country."

Interestingly enough, a significant number (17.2 percent) cited democracy as the best thing about life in Israel (see table 6.1)

Vatikim Success Stories

Despite the difficulties of the initial entry into a new country many Ethiopian immigrants have made a successful life for themselves in Israel. The individuals described below are examples of Ethiopian vatikim who have distinguished themselves in Israeli society.

Meskie Sibru-Siran

Meskie Sibru-Siran is an example of a successful absorption. A 26-year-old actress, singer, and model, she is a symbol of pride and success among Ethiopian women. Meskie came to Israel in 1981 to join her older sister and brother who were living in Tel Aviv. Having a strong interest in acting, she auditioned for several plays in Tel Aviv but was turned down due to her accent. Undaunted, she continued to perform in Amharic as she worked diligently on improving her accent. She was finally admitted into the prestigious Nissan Nativ acting school. After graduation she continued to model, sing, and act. She won a considerable amount of fame when her one-act play, *Song of the Nice Guys*, won third prize in the Theaternetto festival (Sommer 1994).

TABLE 6.1
Best Aspects of Life in Israel

Item	Percentage ($n = 29$)
Religion	10.3
Freedom/Democracy	17.2
Living in my country	24.1
Everything	13.8
Other	17.2
No Response	17.4
Total	100.0

Mulugeta

Ethiopian artist Mulugeta is another success story. He came to Israel on Operation Moses and is poised for fame as a sculptor. Part of a JDC project for immigrant artists, Mulugeta has been assisted with free materials as well as studio space (Bazelon 1993). He was recently chosen as the Israeli representative at a British international sculpture show and is scheduled for a one-man show in Tel Aviv. With his unique talent, he has a bright future.

Addisu Messele

Thirty-seven-year-old Addisu Messele, who is president of the Association of Ethiopian Jews, came to Israel through the Sudan in the 1980s. He is the first Ethiopian immigrant elected to the Knesset. Politically active in Ethiopia, Addisu is the major spokesperson for Beta Israel immigrants in the country (Wagaw 1993). He has defended the religious, political, and social rights of Ethiopian immigrants, seeking recognition for them as social and political equals in Israel.

Addisu is a common sight at the Knesset, conferring with those involved with policy making for immigrants in the country. Since his arrival in Israel, he has been active in placing Ethiopian Jewish issues on the national agenda.

Avraham Nagosa

The story of Avraham Nagosa is told courtesy of JAFI Communications:

> Avraham Nagosa is proud of being the first Ethiopian immigrant to graduate from the Hebrew University as a social worker. Avraham earned his degree after completing four years of study at the Paul Baerwald School of Social Work, during which he received awards and commendations for his volunteerism and field work. Avraham, now in his mid-thirties, came to Israel in 1985 with his wife and small daughter (they have since had another daughter, their first sabra or native-born Israeli). His parents, brothers, and sisters remained in Ethiopia, not knowing that it would be three long years before the family would be reunited in their new home.

Because of his excellent English, Avraham was often called upon to act as an interpreter in his absorption center and helped the social workers understand Ethiopian traditions and culture. Assisted by a Student Authority scholarship, jointly funded by the Jewish Agency and the Ministry of Absorption, Avraham applied for entrance to the one-year preparatory program at Hebrew University's Rothberg School for Overseas Students, the first step toward his chosen vocation. At the end of the one-year preparatory course, Avraham began his professional studies. During the second year of his program, he worked with Ethiopian immigrants at the Hadassah University Hospital's Social Services Department and served as an interpreter in various departments of the hospital, receiving a prize for outstanding service. This success was followed by a year of field work for the Jerusalem Municipality's Department of Social Work in the Gilo neighborhood. His success there was the basis for his being hired by the municipality after graduation.

Avraham is extremely aware of the importance of having Ethiopian social workers in Israel, especially since Operation Solomon, when more than 14,000 Ethiopians were airlifted to Israel. "It is very important that Ethiopian social workers are trained. This will enable better integration of Ethiopian immigrants into Israeli society," Avraham says. "The Ethiopian community has numerous problems, especially with respect to bridging the gap between their culture and the one they find once they arrive. Ethiopian social workers understand the community and speak its language so they can help bridge this gap."

During Operation Solomon, Avraham worked around the clock, greeting the many bewildered new arrivals and explaining the initial procedures. Avraham remembers, "I also had to explain to the Israeli social workers and the workers from the Ministry of Absorption how to approach the Ethiopian immigrants and how to adapt the system to their needs."

Avraham still devotes several hours a week to helping Ethiopian immigrants with their absorption problems. He has helped Ethiopian youngsters in elementary schools to understand the significance of formal education. He was also instrumental in the establishment of the Ethiopian students organization which is open to all Ethiopians studying in postsecondary educational institutions, and he continues to be an active member, stating, "It is important to give Ethiopians the chance to study in the universities, because once they are educated to that standard, they will be able to make a very significant contribution both to their own community and to Israel."

At present, Avraham is content with his task of aiding the elderly with their problems. He feels he is very lucky to be in Israel and is delighted with the course life has taken for him, his wife Leah, who is a nurse at Hadassah Hospital, and their daughters, aged 12 and 2.

Avraham reflects, "Like other groups, the Jews in Ethiopia were allowed to study, serve in the army and if you were qualified, you could work for the government, so on the official level I never felt any anti-Jewish feelings or acts."

He goes on to state, "I see my aliyah as a wonderful event and feel comfortable with the knowledge that my daughters have a wonderful future ahead of them in Israel."

Theodoros Gete

The story of Theodoros Gete is told courtesy of JAFI Communications:

Theodoros Gete is, in his words, "a thousand years" removed from the Jews from the villages of Gondar province, the origin of most of the Ethiopians now living in Israel. Gete, who is 25, comes from Addis Ababa, the modern capital city of over one million inhabitants. In Israel for two years, he now lives in Jerusalem.

Unlike many Ethiopians who have had extended stays in absorption centers, Gete (who is known as "Teddy"), his wife Yerushalayim, and their 6-year-old son Yovel live in a small apartment that resembles the home of an immigrant from North America. Their home, which is sparsely but adequately furnished, has many of the amenities found in most middle-class homes in Israel: television, VCR, microwave oven, and small stereo.

Gete grew up in Addis Ababa, removed from the small Jewish neighborhood, in an area populated mostly by businessmen and civil servants. His father, who speaks five languages, worked in the field of thermal energy but is now employed in the Ethiopian capital by the Israeli embassy.

Teddy Gete's grandfather, Getu Yirmiyahu, was one of two Ethiopian boys taken to Europe by the famous explorer of Ethiopian Jewry, Joseph Halevy, who visited the remote Jewish community at the end of the last century. Yirmiyahu lived and studied in Europe for many years, during which he also visited what was then Palestine; on his return to Ethiopia, he founded a Jewish day school in Gondar.

"I did not grow up in an observant home," Gete says, "but I did grow up with a strong Jewish identity." In contrast, most of the

Jews from the Gondar region are religious, so there are vast cultural differences between them and the Jews from Addis Ababa. Even the Amharic that is spoken is different, according to Gete: "In Gondar they speak the way it was spoken years ago, but in Addis, the language is much more modern." He explains that many words have taken on different nuances and meanings.

"Growing up in Addis, I did not have a lot of Jewish friends," recalls Gete. "Nobody talked about their Jewishness, it was a secret. Even people that lived next door to us for years did not know that we were Jewish. I studied at university with people whom I didn't know were Jews until I met them here in Israel."

Gete arrived in Israel alone in June 1989. Unlike his compatriots, he has relatives in Israel who are well established, including an aunt who has been here for over 40 years.

Nevertheless, Gete's aliyah was not without hardship. He left Ethiopia on the pretense of going to study in the United States and was not permitted to take his wife and son with him. It was ten long months until his family joined him in Jerusalem. Gete explains that under the Marxist regime in Ethiopia at the time, it was a very long and bureaucratic process for anybody to obtain permission to go abroad. Many different authorities, starting with his local neighborhood committee, had to grant approval. If, at any point, any of these committees had said no, that would have been the end of his plans for his future in Israel. Eventually he did receive all of the necessary permits and left Ethiopia for Athens. From Greece, he came to Israel.

Once in Jerusalem, he studied Hebrew at Ulpan Etzion along with other recent immigrants from some 15 countries. He remained there for almost a year, completing beginner and advanced levels of Hebrew studies. Currently, Gete works at an electronics firm in Jerusalem and considers himself lucky to be employed in a field that interests him. Having completed two and half years of a four-year degree in computer science at Addis Ababa University, he plans to continue his studies as soon as possible, depending on finances and his work schedule. In Ethiopia, his wife worked as a project manager for a large construction firm. She now works as a maid at a Jerusalem hotel.

When asked the question that every new immigrant to Israel is asked, "Why did you come?" Gete replies, "I was raised in a Zionist family. Israel was always something that we had talked about. Even though I never met my grandfather, because he died before I was born, his influence was always very strong."

Today in Israel, where one often hears cries of disappointment from the flood of immigrants, Gete is not disappointed. "For me," he says, "Israel has met my expectations."

Tsagai Zaudie

The story of Tsagai Zaudie is told courtesy of JAFI Communications:

In his native Gondar province in Ethiopia, 46-year-old Tsagai Zaudie was a taxi driver. Arriving in Israel nearly a year ago, Zaudie set his sights on driving his own taxi in Israel but did not have the money to buy his own vehicle.

"I've had offers to drive other people's taxis at night," says Zaudie, who has a rugged, furrowed, smiling face, "but I'd rather save up and buy my own taxi. So I enrolled in this building course because I believe there are good employment prospects and salaries in the construction industry."

Zaudie, who lives with his wife and four children at the Jewish Agency's Bet Goldmintz Absorption Center in Netanya, is one of 60 new immigrants from Ethiopia in the Netanya area who are currently participating in a vocational training course designed for the building industry. All of these construction apprentices come from four different Jewish Agency absorption centers. Their mornings are spent studying Hebrew at an *ulpan* (language training school) and from two until five in the afternoon they attend the Construction Technological College, sponsored by Israel's Ministry of Labor and Social Welfare. Here, Zaudie is specializing in laying foundations, while others learn about plastering walls and laying floor tiles.

Ya'akov Ben Tal, the director of the Construction Technological College, is very pleased with his students. "They are enthusiastic, punctual, very hard-working and good-natured," he says. The course includes a two-month apprenticeship with hand-picked contractors who are sensitive to the culture shock problems confronting the newcomers from Ethiopia. When the students graduate, they will all find employment among the major and small construction companies, including Solel Boneh, that regularly hire the graduates of the college.

According to Yona Dotan, the Jewish Agency's educational and cultural coordinator at the Bet Goldmintz Absorption Center in Netanya, all the Ethiopians will successfully conclude the course. "Some may take longer than the usual 60 days to reach the required standard," she concedes, "but these will receive extra tuition until they have attained the necessary level and pass the exams required to receive their government certificates."

Dotan's greatest concern is that many of the newcomers from Ethiopia are too naive and honest for the rough, tough, competitive world of construction. "No doubt, in the future, certain unscrupulous contractors will try to exploit their honest, hard-working ways," she says. "It's a tough world and they'll have to learn the hard way."

Zaudie, who considered several options before selecting the course at the Construction Technological College, has no illusions about what awaits him. "We Ethiopians are gentle, easygoing people," he asserts. "But we know how to look after ourselves. We watch out for each other as well. We want good money and we are prepared to work for it. We won't let anybody cheat us."

Also attending the construction course is fellow Ethiopian Agegnehu Attallalu, who is 26. Like Zaudie, he lives presently in the comfort of the Bet Goldmintz Absorption Center. Yet he is acutely conscious that he will soon have to take responsibility for his own future in Israel.

"Everything is happening to me at once," laughs Attallalu with an infectious smile. "Since reaching Israel last year I have got married and now we are expecting our first child. By the summer we'll be in the outside world on our own without the shelter of the Jewish Agency. This course offers me the opportunity to make a good salary."

Zaudie agrees wholeheartedly. "With so many immigrants flooding into the country from Ethiopia and Russia," he says, "There has to be plenty of work in construction. In effect you could say we will be building homes for ourselves and our community."

David Mehrate

The story of David Mehrate is told courtesy of JAFI Communications:

David Mehrate, a 23-year-old new Ethiopian immigrant, recently received the "Special Communal Services Award" from Knesset Speaker Dov Shilansky. He was selected for this citation from the thousands of new immigrant students who receive grants from the Jewish Agency's Student Authority and in return are expected to devote several hours a week to voluntary work.

Mehrate chose to spend an entire day each week at the Jewish Agency's Kiryat Gat Absorption Center offering the Ethiopian immigrants there the benefit of his six years' experience in Israel. "I translate documents for them," he explains, "fill in forms, and accompany the immigrants to government offices. Most importantly, I can give them encouragement and advice. I understand the culture shock and the need to adjust perspectives that aliyah causes."

Mehrate has himself overcome the culture shock admirably. A third-year student in Industrial Engineering and Management at Beersheba's College of Technology, he admits that he is fascinated by modern technology. "Perhaps this is because of the absence of modern technology in Weleka, my native village in Gondar province in Ethiopia," he says.

Mehrate reached Israel in 1984 with his parents, brother, and sister. Two more brothers still remain in Ethiopia unable to leave. This is a source of great sorrow to Mehrate who tells of his parents' deep anguish about the matter. His parents, who both worked as farmers in Ethiopia and now live in Kiryat Gat, have never really adjusted to life in Israel.

So Mehrate, as the eldest of his parents' three children in Israel, has had to assume a leadership role. Consequently, he is mature and responsible for his age and is used to giving rather than taking. It is this mixture of kindness, conscientiousness and sense of duty to the community that earned him the Communal Service Award.

"I felt proud when I went to the Knesset," Mehrate recalls. "Like all Jews we Ethiopians have always yearned to be in Jerusalem. And there I was in the very bastion of Jewish sovereignty and democracy. I felt proud not only for myself but for my family and the entire Ethiopian Jewish community." When Mehrate graduates from college later this year he will be inducted into the Israeli Defense Force where he hopes to be able to use his engineering skills.

He has found minimal discrimination since being in Israel although he laughs that many Israelis do not know where Ethiopia is on the map and are not always sensitive to the problems confronting Ethiopian immigrants. "But I am the only Ethiopian in my class at college," he says, "and when I'm with all my friends there I feel like a regular Israeli."

An observant rather than an orthodox Jew, Mehrate attends Shabbat services at a nearby Moroccan synagogue. "I would be more comfortable in Beersheba's Ethiopian synagogue," he hastens to add, "but it is too far to walk there."

"When I finish the army, I would like to settle in Kiryat Gat near my parents," he says, "providing of course that I can find a suitable job. I like living in the south of Israel. It is important for me to stay close to my family. I feel like an Israeli but my Ethiopian Jewish roots are also an integral part of my identity. All of us are not complete without our past as well as our future."

Chapter 7

The Absorption Process

Recently arrived Ethiopian immigrants are generally placed in hotels converted into absorption centers. It is in these centers that they begin the process of adapting to Israeli society. The following example of the absorption process for immigrants of Operation Moses in the 1980s is described by Barry Weise (1991), former director of immigration, the National Jewish Community Relations Advisory Council:

The process of absorption begins shortly after a new immigrant's arrival in Israel. Upon arrival, they are interviewed by Jewish Agency workers to determine their family status and medical needs. The interviews are conducted by teams of social workers and veteran Israeli Ethiopian *madrichim* (instructors). They organize the immigrants into family units, attempting to place children and elderly immigrants who have been separated from their families with other relatives in Israel. Some are hospitalized immediately; the rest are taken to absorption centers around the country. In the following days, medical treatment administered by the Ministry of Health begins. Nearly every immigrant is ill from one tropical ailment or another. Malaria, tuberculosis, pneumonia, and intestinal parasites are commonly found. Youngsters and even some adults arrive wearing rags; children under five sometimes come wearing nothing at all. At the Jewish Agency's absorption centers they are given food and clothes and are assigned to their new apartments. Paraprofessionals called *somchot* immediately begin to teach the new immigrants how to properly use gas stoves and electrical appliances.

Relatives from all over the country learn of the new arrivals and flock to the absorption center. During the first few days the new

Israelis are left alone to be with their relatives to rest and to adjust to being in Israel.

During the first four to six weeks, the new immigrants learn the basics of dealing with life in a modern society: how to use money, go shopping, and open a bank account, and so forth. Medical care continues throughout this period. Informal classes are conducted introducing them to Hebrew, Jewish history, and Israeli culture and society.

At the end of the initial acclimatization period, the Ministry of Education begins formal classes in Hebrew at the ulpan. Except for a limited number of young people who have received upwards of twelve years of education in Ethiopia, most Ethiopian immigrants come with no formal educational background. Training at the ulpan lasts half a year during which time the new immigrants are expected to learn to read, write, and speak basic Hebrew. In addition to training them in Hebrew, the ulpan also provides instructions in government, modern Israeli culture, and rituals according to traditional rabbinic practice. Children learn Hebrew quickly and are placed in classes with other Israelis in school. All immigrant children from Ethiopia attend religious schools. Older children learn in special classes for Ethiopian immigrants.

Unstable conditions in Ethiopia and in the border refugee camps have brought about the arrival in Israel of hundreds of children without their parents. These children, who are under the care of the Youth Aliyah Department of the Jewish Agency, live in Youth Aliyah villages designed to deal with the special needs of young immigrants who come to Israel alone. Young Ethiopian immigrants who have finished several years of elementary and secondary education in Ethiopia are placed in special absorption centers to prepare them for postsecondary education. These centers are created to bridge the gap between the educational levels of Ethiopian and Israeli students.

Most adult immigrants begin a vocational course of study designed to retrain them for life in modern Israel by acquainting them with the basic skills necessary for success. In addition to arithmetic, intermediate Hebrew, and technical terminology, basic work habits and familiarity with machine parts are taught. At the conclusion of the vocational course, the immigrant decides if he will continue on to a professional training course or if he will go directly to the Israeli workforce. Those who decide to go directly to work are aided in finding jobs by a representative of the Ministry of Labor. The social workers also ensure that jobs with promise are found. In most cases the immigrants are placed in factory jobs that include hands-on training and possibilities for advancement. Although Ethiopian Jews have been in Israel only a short period of time, they have already established a reputation for being dedicated and hard-working employees.

Those who decide to train for a profession continue in courses that last from a few months to a year. All those who are able are encouraged to go on to professional training. Courses offered enable them to become electricians, automobile body workers, carpenters, garage mechanics, plumbers, seamstresses, beauticians, and so forth. Lessons in the Hebrew language also continue during the training. At the conclusion of the course, the graduates are given certificates of completion and are aided in job placement.

After finishing formal studies at the ulpan and a vocational or professional course, most immigrants leave the absorption center and move to rent-subsidized apartments. Representatives of the Housing Ministry aid them in their efforts to secure an apartment. The apartments are located in development towns, usually in complexes near other Ethiopian immigrants to promote mutual support systems, creating cluster formations. To avoid the formation of ghettos, the clusters are interspersed within areas where Israelis from other parts of the world are living.

In order to ease the transition from life in the absorption center to independent living outside of the center, early on in the absorption process the social workers plan projects to promote contact with non-Ethiopian Israelis. The "home hospitality" program with veteran Israeli families is one such project. Ethiopian immigrants are also encouraged to take part in programs offered by local community centers. Finally, day-to-day contact with other Israelis at the store, bank, or government ministries increases as the months pass.

The immigrants' integration is also helped by government efforts to educate the general Israeli populace about them. As Ethiopian Jews are brought to a new town, meetings are held with various municipal officials to acquaint them with the special needs of Ethiopian immigrants. Also, public meetings are held to educate the general community about the new residents of the town. Lectures are given by the social workers and veteran Israeli Ethiopians about the history and culture of Ethiopian Jews. In many towns the result has been very successful, with public events welcoming the new immigrants and volunteer efforts to aid them in their absorption needs. Finally, special Kabbalat Shabbat and other events are organized by the community so that Ethiopian Jews may join them for the holiday celebration.

Family Life in the Absorption Centers

Absorption centers traditionally were built to house immigrants while they learned to speak the language and adjust to Israeli society. After a period of one year, it was expected that they would be employed and settled in the community. Due to the economic pressures brought on by large waves of immigrants to Israel, however, absorption centers no longer function in the same manner. Most immigrants are absorbed directly into the community, with the exception of Ethiopians and some Soviet immigrants, who are placed in hotels or mobile homes.

During the period of this study, 97.7 percent of the Ethiopian olim interviewed were living in absorption centers, and only one (2.3 percent) lived elsewhere; 61.1 percent were in hotels, 16.3 percent in caravans, and 18.6 percent were reluctant to identify where they lived. Among the vatikim, 75.9 percent reported living in an absorption center after their arrival in Israel.

The Jewish Agency (1992) reported 24,750 Ethiopians in absorption processes, of whom 5,651 were in 10 caravan sites, 11,397 in hotels, and 7,202 in absorption centers. There are also 2,770 children in Youth Aliya frameworks (boarding schools). Our study found that hotel and caravan absorption centers placed a strain on family relationships, and in some cases they modified the family structure. In addition, the center detracted from the absorption process by isolating the immigrants from the Israeli community.

The Hotel Shalom, located on the periphery of Jerusalem, is typical of absorption center hotels in Israel. Due to the shortage of traditional centers, Ethiopian immigrants who arrived via Operation Solomon were hastily placed in hotels like Hotel Shalom, which were leased from private owners. At the hotel, services such as food and maintenance are provided by the staff, and each family is given a room(s). Everyone eats in a central dining room. A small monthly stipend is paid by the Jewish Agency to olim for other needs. The staff of the Jewish Agency administers the centers, and several different groups of immigrants may live there. The Hotel Shalom, for example, is occupied by both Ethiopian and Soviet immigrants.

Absorption center life has caused family bonds to weaken, as families live in different rooms and cannot interact in a normal fashion. The traditional roles of both males and females have been altered; for example, fathers are no longer the breadwinners, and mothers do not perform the routine cleaning and cooking for the family as before. The authority figure for the children no longer is the father but the center's director, who makes the final decision on most matters concerning life in the absorption center. For example, a child on the verge of being spanked warned his father that he would tell the caravan director. Ethiopian society is patriarchal, and this incident illustrates how the distribution of power in the family is shifted and the father's position as an authority figure challenged. Wife-beating occasionally occurs as a response to attempts by some women to assert their independence in the new, more liberal environment of Israel. The children of the absorption center live in two worlds: they are torn between traditional values and the new Israeli society. Exposed to new demands placed on them at school and in the community, they grapple with balancing dual responsibilities and harmonizing cultural differences.

Few supports are given to immigrant families in terms of their emotional and psychological needs while living in absorption centers. On November 29, 1991, an immigrant from Ethiopia murdered his wife and then killed himself in an absorption center near Mikhssoret (Greenwood 1992). Food, clothing, and material needs are adequately provided, yet few centers employ Ethiopian social workers or psychologists, and there is only one Beta Israel psychiatrist in Israel. The Israeli social workers interviewed did not speak Amharic, the language of the immigrants, so they depend on absorption center translators. In addition, social workers are too heavily burdened with helping immigrants get through the bureaucracy to have adequate time for counseling and other traditional social work functions.

Isolation from the Israeli community is perhaps the greatest drawback to living in an absorption center hotel or caravan, as there are few opportunities to interact with the community. The Hulda caravan site, for example, is located miles away from the nearest town and far away from Jerusalem, the closest major city.

Hulda caravan site is occupied solely by Ethiopians, with more than 1,000 residents. Although the mobile homes have electricity, pipe-borne water, and 24-hour security, each is much too small for a typical Ethiopian family. Families are thus allocated more than one unit, separating family members from each other. Transportation is available on buses that take children to school and residents to town. Some of the residents have saved their allowances (at the expense of their daily needs) to buy televisions and VCRs. Other than members of the Jewish Agency or tradesmen from town, Israelis are rarely seen visiting the caravans. It appears that interactions on a social level are virtually nonexistent among caravan members and townspeople.

Some caravans are occupied by both Soviet and Ethiopian immigrants, but they live in different parts of the grounds, with virtually no social interaction except on a superficial level. Soviet and Ethiopian children play together, but adults keep their distance.

Isolation caused by lack of transportation was such a problem in the Galilee that Ethiopian immigrants called a strike at the Kadoorie mobile home site. The protesters complained that they had to walk over half a kilometer to the nearest bus stop in Kfar Tavor, and this, they said, was particularly dangerous at night ("Ethiopian immigrants" July 15, 1992).

Another protest erupted in Givat Napoleon when Ethiopian caravan families prevented Jewish Agency staff from entering their offices and refused to send their youngsters to school because they felt they were being "deprived" of money. While the charges by the olim proved groundless, lack of communication between Jewish Agency officials and Ethiopian families resulted in a misunderstanding that could have been avoided if Ethiopian olim had been adequately informed.

Perhaps most problematic among absorption center residents are immigrants who come without their families or who have left significant others behind in Ethiopia. For example, a respondent related the case of a father of four who left his wife and children in Ethiopia. When he did not receive satisfactory answers from Jewish Agency officials as to their whereabouts, he became severely depressed and threatened suicide. Words of comfort and encouragement from other residents prevented a tragedy from happening before his family arrived 11 months later.

Among the immigrants are also a number of single parents, most often women with children. They represent a family unit most in need of economic support once government subsidies cease. The story of two immigrants, an Ethiopian and a Soviet women as told to a family psychologist, Professor Amith Ben-David of Haifa University best illustrate the problems of single parents. The first is Burtukan, an immigrant from Ethiopia, the second Larissa, an immigrant from Latvia.

Burtukan's Story

In 1991 I came to Israel. In Israel it is good, but in Ethiopia it was good too. I do not work. I receive payment from Social Security. When I move from the caravan, I will have to work. Now only the men work. We don't know how to work here, so we receive money from the government. In Ethiopia there was lots of work. We had to work at home. Here there is almost no work to do. I have to cook and clean. In Ethiopia I had to sew and prepare some jewelry also. Here I have to help my sister when she needs me; like last week when her youngest son was sick and in the hospital, I took care of her other children and prepared the food for them. Usually she helps me, since she is so much older than I am. Here in the city we are two, my sister and I. In the country there are five of us, and our parents live here too, but far away. In Ethiopia my sister was a storyteller, but here she can't do it since she knows no Hebrew.

When we came to this country, we lived in Ayelet Hashachar. There I became pregnant. It was good there. We worked in the fields and with the cattle. I took out a carrot from the earth and ate it. I remember I ate a lot because I was pregnant and was very hungry. I was married by Ethiopian law, but according to Israeli law I am not married. My husband left me when I was five months pregnant. He was no good. He didn't want to live with me. I have no idea where he is now. If he wants to come and live with me, then he is welcome. I don't know why he left me.

I don't know what he has in his head and in his heart. I don't love him. There are many women here who have no husband. If I want to get married again, I can marry whoever I want and as many times as I want. But here in Israel it is different. People say that if somebody left you, then you are no good, and another man will not want to take me. I want to get married again, but it is hard to find a good husband. My mother says that she doesn't want me to be like my sister who got married four times and was left four times by her husbands. She says that once is enough.

The hardest thing is that I do not know how to work; also that I am alone. If I get sick, who will help me? My sister will take care of my food and clothes. Last time I saw my parents was about five months ago. I haven't worked in a year and seven months, and I am worried because I don't know how to work. If Social Security stops paying, I don't know what I will do. I am worried because the caravan where I live is damaged and rats get into it, and I have to keep them away all the time. I have to ask somebody to help me fix the floor; I sometimes do it and a man comes and helps.

My son . . . goes to the nursery from eight till three and then I take care of him. He is now a year and a half and I still nurse him. In Ethiopia you eat a lot and then you have a lot of milk, so you nurse the children until late. He is my first, but I want to have more and have them live with me. I send him to the nursery because there they teach him good manners. He comes home and he is a terror. It is hard to take care of him without a father. I try to talk to him and I sometimes shout at him, but I try not to hit him. To be a single mother is hard. Money is a problem. If they stop paying, I don't know what I will do. A working single mother has a more difficult time because she has to pick up her son immediately after work, and she hardly manages. Here it is difficult. In Ethiopia it was easier. But I am still happy I am here. My life here is good but I still cry a lot because I am far from my family and I miss them. A family is the most important thing in life.

Burtukan came to Israel via a concentrated governmental effort to rescue all the remaining Ethiopian Jews before the political events in Ethiopia made it impossible to leave the country. Burtukan came as a refugee and her life was determined by administrative decisions regarding where and with whom she should live. She was left, soon after arriving, without the immediate family with whom she had been used to living and is now in the process of creating a new life for herself. It is clear from her story how lonely, lost, and dislocated she feels and how much she wants to feel the earth (the rural life) under her feet, like in Ethiopia or even in Ayelet Hashachar where she worked in the fields and with the livestock. The feeling Burtukan conveys in her story is the total dependence on government support. Burtukan explains that the way she has been taught how to earn a living is not adequate here. She will have to learn how to work before she can look for a job. Meanwhile, she does everything possible to fulfill her job of taking care of her son and helping her sister.

Burtukan talks about her past with a longing for a time when the roles, the rules, and the relationships were clear. She knew how to work, where to find her parents and brothers and sisters, what the rules about marriage and divorce were, and what her future would be. Burtukan refers here to one of the main concerns of the Ethiopian family. Marriages are conducted in Ethiopia by the spiritual leader, the kess. According to the Israeli laws governing marriage, only the religious law is binding. According to Jewish religious law, it is much more difficult to divorce and get remarried. This is one of Burtukan's concerns, and she stresses that since she was married by a kess, her marriage is not recognized here, thus affording her the opportunity of getting married again without further complications.

Burtukan talks about her son as the person who will not be taken away from her. He is the only one over whom she has some kind of control. He is like an extension of herself and she feels secure because of him. The issue of the color of his skin is interesting: She refers here to the fact that her son's skin is lighter than her own. Many Ethiopian immigrants have referred to the fact that they were unaware in Ethiopia of the existence of people with a skin color different than theirs. A girl once wrote in a poem: "Mother, in Ethiopia you were white, and here you are black." Burtukan here expresses the wish that her son will look more like the white majority in Israel, rather than black.

Larissa's Story

We came to Israel a year and a half ago—myself, my daughter, and my boyfriend. I am glad I immigrated, however difficult it is here. Up until a few months ago, my boyfriend lived with us, but then we separated. I think I am no good with men. I left my former husband when my daughter was a year and a half old. She almost doesn't remember him, since I moved back to Latvia to live with my parents.

Here I have a difficult time with the child alone. There is nobody to help. I have an uncle and an aunt here in Israel and they come to visit quite often, but they cannot give me any money, and so I completely depend on the money from Social Security. I did not expect to receive any help here; I know that I would have to manage by myself, I knew it when I decided I wanted to divorce my ex-husband, and I knew it when I decided to separate from my boyfriend. He wasn't so helpful with my daughter. If I have to go out, I have here some neighbors, older people, who help me with her.

Sometimes I have to leave her alone when I have to go out, but she is a good child; she can see I am going through some rough times, and she tries to help.

The most difficult problem I have now is money. Nobody wants to give work to a new immigrant who is alone with a small child. That is the toughest problem. The other issue that I am worried about is that my little daughter has to stay alone at home. She opens the door, and you have no idea what kind of dangerous people move around here. The social worker came to tell us that there is a young boy here that bothers little girls. I told her and explained to her about him. She has to know what is going on in the world around her. I hope she doesn't open the door now.

In Russia life was good; everything was good there. So, you ask, why am I here? Well, I have some relatives here, and besides, right now life is very difficult there. My mother was left there with my sister. My father passed away six years ago. My mother will come when my personal and economic situation improves. I cannot help her right now, so there is no point in her coming. Maybe next year I will be able to get myself an apartment and then she can come and live with me. My older sister will never come; her husband is not Jewish and is very successful there. He will never come here.

When my mother comes, it will be easier because there will be one more person to help with my daughter. In Russia it is much easier because there are nurseries from early in the morning till late evening, so children are taken care of all day; you pay very little and can work all day. Besides, my mother helped me a lot. In Russia there are many women who raise their children alone and there is nothing strange about it. Here I think people talk behind my back. The only difficulty I encounter is that I cannot get a job because I have to be home at around one o'clock when my daughter gets home from school. However, I am glad I have her. She is a good child; she is smart and has a good and gentle disposition. She usually agrees with me not only because she thinks like me, but because she understands the situation and knows it is difficult.

I am glad we are here; I have relatives, and there is a future here. You know that if you want to get things, there is a chance that you will be able to get them. I want to study some more. Maybe when my mother comes, I will be able to go and learn design, and I will be able to work designing clothes and later do some sewing and earn more money. I am not sure if I will ever get married again. I don't think about it now. I only think about making a better life for me and my daughter. I had so many problems with my ex-husband and my boyfriend. Maybe I am not good at it at all.

Larissa chose to emigrate and leave her mother behind. Her independence and amount of control stand out in relation to her situation and to her future. She states that it was her choice t̲ leave her husband, as it was her choice to immigrate to Israel and leave her family. Since she came to Israel, she also chose to leave her boyfriend and return to the state she knows best: being with her daughter, alone.

Her state of transition still dominates, and she conveys the feeling of being in an unsettled time, in which she is uncertain as to the future. She has not resolved many of the issues ahead of her. She still reminisces about her past and has idealized the better aspects of life in the former Soviet Union, such as the affordable all-day nurseries that took care of her little girl and gave her the opportunity to work. It is well known that the government wanted to offer good child care so that mothers could work. She also remembers the feeling from the past, of being part of the culture, of not being different. She states that in Russia, there were many women in single-parent families, unlike in Israel. This feeling of being different, of not belonging, is typical of immigrants, especially during the initial adjustment period. Russian immigrants say that in Russia they were considered Jews, and here in Israel they are considered Russians. This tells the tale of the immigrant who feels strange and on the fringe of the majority culture.

Larissa speaks about her daughter with enthusiasm. She sees in her a companion and feels she must invest in her as much as she can. She wants her to be a good student and to be able to stand up for herself. She feels she has to watch over her, and what matters most is not disciplining but protecting her. Larissa's future will have to include some kind of job; that is her primary concern for the present. However, she feels that she will not be able to get a job unless her personal situation changes. She seems to be at a point where there are more questions than answers, regarding a place to live, a job, and her relationship with men.

Epilogue

The stories of Burtukan and Larissa are their way of giving meaning to their lives across time. Simultaneously, the stories are a way of learning about the meaning they give to their experiences. Burtukan and Larissa talk about themselves, their families, and their children in relation to the premigratory period (their past), the postmigratory period (their present), and their future. Learn-

ɔf these two women through their narratives
ɑpse into their world in order to understand the
ɪe changes facing both of them in the process of

.d Larissa arrived in Israel at about the same time. Both ᴰᵁᴵ. ɪ and Larissa worry about money and making ends meet. This is typical of almost all single-mother families. In spite of the similarities in the life cycle of both Burtukan and Larissa, there are obvious cultural differences that stem from different childrearing practices, perceptions of the functions and responsibilities of extended family, and expectations from future generations. These differences are overshadowed by the process of absorption in a new country, in which they are both faced with the same tasks: finding adequate jobs and integrating into a new social structure (Richards and Schmiege 1993). Job training and special programs for single parents as soon as they arrive in Israel would help, so that single-parent families will not become dependent on the welfare system.

A program of support for single Soviet mothers called the Women's Career Monitoring Project was initiated by an Israeli social worker, Judy Fierstein. Funded by the Joint Distribution Committee, professional immigrant single women were matched up with Israeli women in the same or a similar field who could act as mentors to the newcomers ("Israeli career women" 1991). A similar program should be started for Ethiopian single mothers.

The Elderly

Another special group is the Ethiopian elderly. Several of the olim interviewed were of retirement age and arrived as members of an extended family. Due to their advanced age, they were not actively seeking work but living on government pension; yet finding a role in an entirely new society was hard.

Elderly vatikim, most particularly, found learning Hebrew difficult and often they were separated from their adult children who were serving in the military or working in other parts of the country. The fast pace of Israeli industrial society, in combination with the uncertainty of a new life at an older age, made absorption difficult.

Ethiopian Immigrants' Perception of the Absorption Center

Ethiopian immigrants were asked questions about their experiences at the absorption center. Olim were asked how the program at the absorption center was helping them. As shown in table 7.1, about a third of the olim reported that they were helped with food and accommodations (16.5 percent) or money (16.5 percent), while 4 percent said the ulpan was useful. About 60 percent said the absorption center was not helpful at all. For one of the olim, the question was not relevant, as he lived in a youth hostel. Several of the immigrants complained that they were unaccustomed to the food served in the absorption center and decided to prepare their own meals.

Vatikim were asked about their experiences in absorption centers. When they were asked the positive aspects of the absorption center, the majority of vatikim who had experienced life in an absorption center said there was nothing good about their life there. This accounted for 25 percent of the sample. Twenty-one percent of the sample said that "everything" at the absorption center was positive. As can be seen in table 7.2, "social life" and the "staff" accounted for one-fourth of the responses, while numerous other responses were given by the remaining vatikim. There appeared to be a great deal of ambivalence among vatikim about absorption center life.

The vatikim also were asked what they considered the worst

TABLE 7.1
Olim Perceptions of Positive Aspects of the Absorption Center

Item	Percentage (n = 43)
No help	60.0
Food and shelter	16.5
Money	16.5
Ulpan	04.0
Not applicable	03.0
Total	100.0

TABLE 7.2
Vatikim Perceptions of Positive Aspects of the Absorption Center

Item	Percentage ($n = 29$)
Nothing good	25
Everything good	21
Social life	13
The staff	13
Physical environment	04
Free-of-charge	04
Do not know	08
No Response	04
Other	08
Total	100

aspect of the absorption center. As shown in table 7.3, 55 percent said there was nothing bad about the center. Food was the response given by 6.9 percent, and numerous other reasons were given by 10.3 percent of the sample.

Olim had experienced a number of problems since immigration. Language (62.8 percent) was the problem most often mentioned, 9.3 percent said housing, 2.3 percent said unemployment,

TABLE 7.3
Vatikim Perceptions of Worst Aspects of the Absorption Center

Item	Percentage ($n = 29$)
Nothing bad	55.0
Food	06.9
Other reasons	10.3
No Response	27.8
Total	100.0

Note: This question was not applicable to 5 of the vatikim, who had never lived in an absorption enter.

and 18.6 percent gave a number of other reasons such as money, food, and culture shock (see table 7.4). Olim also were asked what kind of help they were getting for their problems. In response 36 percent said they were getting no help, an equal number said they were helped by attending language classes at the ulpan, while 8 percent gave numerous other reasons, and 5 percent said occasional work was helpful (see table 7.5).

The data suggest that Ethiopian immigrants are ambivalent about the usefulness of absorption centers because the programs do not help them much with the problems of adjustment. The language training obtained at the ulpan was perceived by the immigrants as the only useful program at the absorption center.

TABLE 7.4
Olim Perceptions of Problems Since Immigration

Item	Percentage ($n = 43$)
Language	62.8
Housing	09.3
Unemployment	02.3
Other (food, culture shock, etc.)	18.6
No response	07.0
Total	100.0

TABLE 7.5
Olim Perceptions of Assistance With Problems

Item	Percentage ($n = 43$)
No help	36.0
Ulpan	36.0
Occasional work	05.0
Other	08.0
No response	15.0
Total	100.0

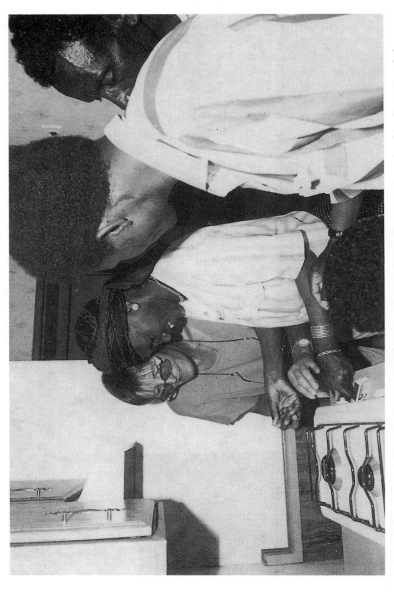

A Jewish Agency social worker shows an Ethiopian housewife (center), newly arrived in Operation Solomon, how to light the gas stove in the kitchen of her caravan-home in the Galilee. (Paul Samson/JAFI)

Ethiopian youngsters who arrived during Operation Solomon in front of their caravan-homes in the Bet Shean Valley. (Paul Samson/JAFI Communications)

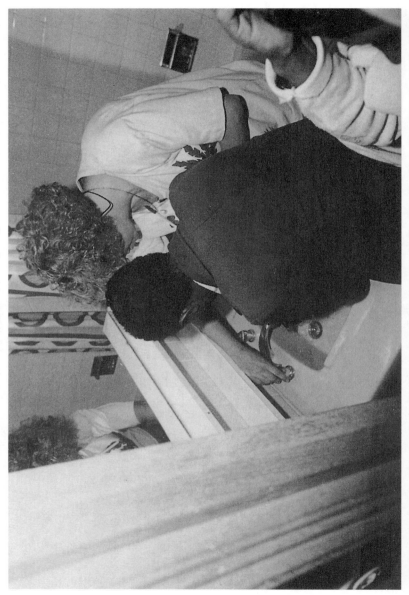

A volunteer (right) shows a newcomer from Ethiopia in Operation Solomon the use of the hot water tap in the

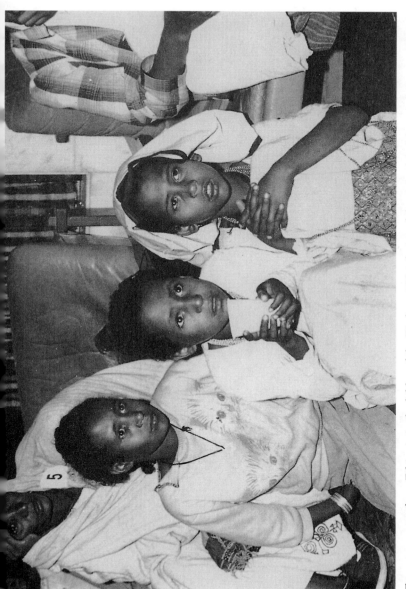

The newcomers from Ethiopia in the lobby of the Diplomat Hotel, one of the many hotels around the country converted by the Jewish Agency into an absorption center to accommodate the arrival of more than 14,000 Jews in Operation Solomon. (Paul Samson/JAFI Communications)

Chapter 8

Absorption Concerns

Unlike other immigrants, except for the Yemenites, the Ethiopians arrived in Israel with some striking differences. The first is skin color. Sociologists theorize that skin color is a consideration for social distancing of one social group from another, and in predominantly white societies it is black skin that is the basis for exclusion (Schaefer 1993).

A study by psychologists Munitz, Priel, and Hernik (1987) comparing Israeli and Ethiopian-born children found that both types of children preferred light-skinned to dark-skinned figures and that Ethiopian preschool children experienced self-color misidentification. That is, they perceived themselves as white.

Goldberg and Kirschenbaum (1989), in a study of the attitudes of white Israelis toward black newcomers, found that few Israelis objected to most types of social relationships with Ethiopian Jews, with the exception of primary group (family) relationships. Yet it is through the primary group that the degree of acceptance of the black newcomers can best be judged, and it is at this level of social interaction that Ethiopian immigrants are least accepted. It appears that skin color is important when considering the absorption of Ethiopian Jews and is a factor that should be examined in more depth.

Second, Ethiopian Jews differ from other immigrant groups (e.g., Soviet Jews) because they arrive with skills more suited to a peasant agrarian society than to a modern state like Israel. They are similar in some ways to Sephardic (Oriental) Jews, who came to Israel from Middle Eastern Arabic countries in the 1950s and took jobs as laborers and blue-collar workers. According to Yonah

(1991), Sephardic Jews seeking acceptance in Israel were faced with prejudices based on the stereotype that the Arabic culture and values that they exhibited were antiquated, backward, and primitive.

Will this be the fate of the newly arrived Ethiopian Jews in Israel? A study by Halper (1987) compared the process of absorption of Jews from Middle Eastern countries during the 1950s with present-day Ethiopian immigrants. Halper found that some of the errors of the past were being repeated with the new immigrant population. One was lack of sensitivity by the authorities to the cultural background of Ethiopians. If this is true, then what effect will the policy of assimilation have on the customs and lifestyles of newly arrived Ethiopian immigrants, and how will this enhance or distract from the absorption process?

Last, many of the Falashas' religious customs are different from those of mainstream Jewry—the most notable being marriage rites. Isolated from the Jewish community for years, Ethiopian Jews centered their faith on the Torah alone. They were led by kessem (priests) rather than rabbis. Also, the prayer book of the Ethiopian Jews is written in Ge'ez rather than Hebrew, another difference from mainstream Jewish religious practice. Absorption may require the relinquishing of many ancient traditions and religious customs by Ethiopian immigrants and, in some ways, a lessening of their cultural identity. The effect this will have on Ethiopian families' adaptation to Israeli life is a major factor that should be examined and a central theme of this study.

In order to successfully integrate Ethiopian Jews into Israeli society, it is necessary to take cognizance of the experiences of the past. The experience of those Ethiopian Jews who have been successfully "absorbed" should be documented and the lessons learned shared with social workers, government officials, and others working with new immigrant populations. Absorption from the viewpoint of the immigrant must be examined and the expectations and aspirations of newly arrived black Jews given consideration when planning for their future in Israel.

The Ethiopian Immigrants Speak for Themselves: Case Studies of Ethiopian Jews

The survey data clearly show the similarities of Ethiopian olim as they begin the absorption process in Israel. These data also describe the similar experiences of the vatikim Ethiopians. What the survey data do not present is the individual differences of the group and the diversity found within. Yet the micro level of research is important for understanding a social phenomenon (Williams 1991).

In order to take into account individual differences, case histories were taken of each Ethiopian immigrant who participated in the study. In-depth interviews were focused on the following areas:

1. Experiences in Ethiopia and reaching Israel
2. Problems encountered since arrival
3. Aspiration for life in Israel

The interviews were unstructured and free-flowing; however, the interviewers were trained to focus all questions in the three designated areas. Each interview took about sixty minutes for completion and commenced immediately after the personality-administered questionnaire was completed. Information was recorded on a blank sheet of the questionnaire, and all interviews were sorted into five categories for analysis: male heads-of-household, female heads of household, single females, single males, and the aged.

The cases are analyzed from the perspective of assessing the social service needs of the family. Social workers with Ethiopian Jewish clients can use aggregate statistics to understand their client population better; however, social work intervention strategies based on these case histories may be useful in day-to-day practice.

Typical cases of Ethiopian immigrants are presented and appropriate social service plans given. Because this study was cross-sectional rather than longitudinal, the interventions were not applied and their outcomes not measured; yet the approaches described may be useful to social workers as a frame of reference for developing similar social service plans for the Ethiopian client population.

Male Heads of Household

Case 5

Subject 5 is a fifty-seven-year-old, Ethiopian, male head of household who came to Israel in Operation Moses, May 1991. He was accompanied by his wife and ten children (three girls and seven boys). Since their arrival, they have resided in an absorption center hotel.

Born in Gondar province, the subject is an animal breeder and a farmer by trade and was pursuing these vocations until he was conscripted into the Ethiopian army, where he served 13 years before he deserted. Since his arrival in Israel, he has been unemployed because he does not know Hebrew well, his skills are inappropriate for the marketplace, and he is physically disabled. He sustained a serious injury to the hand while serving in the army, so his prospects for work are limited.

He reports that he has faced numerous problems in Israel, most particularly culture shock. He sees the need for permanent housing as the most serious concern of his large family. He has no friends or extended family members in Israel. Therefore, the government and voluntary agencies are his only means of social support. Despite these disadvantages, he was very positive about the future. He felt that coming to Israel was the best thing for his family and that their condition is far better than what it was in Ethiopia.

Subject 5 in many ways typifies olim heads of households who come to Israel. Employment and adequate housing are immediate problems for the family while language difficulties and culture shock compound the problems of assimilation. Lack of adequate social services to address the needs of unemployed heads of household makes overcoming these problems even more difficult. All are common problems found among the immigrant families in Israel. The uniqueness of this case, however, is the size of the family and immigrant's physical disabilities.

The medical needs of this client should be addressed immediately and an assessment made of the extent of his disability and the need for vocational rehabilitation services. A work assessment is crucial to determine if he has any likelihood of employment after rehabilitation or whether a sheltered workshop setting will be required. Language difficulties can be dealt with in the ulpan classes, and intense counseling for the man and his family with social workers will help them overcome the tremendous cultural shock brought on by their move to Israeli society.

The large size of the family will affect every aspect of their lives in Israel. The need for more resources, including spacious housing, will put more pressure on the head of household for immediate employment. The role the wife can play in assuming some of the economic responsibility should be explored including training for employment outside of the home.

During the family's adjustment period, material and psychological supports, guided wisely by governmental agencies, would help them make a meaningful transition and facilitate the role of the father as breadwinner and head of the family.

Case 10

Subject 10 is a forty-two-year-old Ethiopian male whose family remained behind in Ethiopia. He is married and the father of six children. He has no formal education and earned a living in Ethiopia as a farmer and metal-worker. He has been a resident of an absorption center for four months.

Since his arrival he has had numerous problems, the most significant being the absence of his family. He did not explain why he failed to bring his family along, but he says he misses his wife and six children (ages one to eleven years old) very much. At one point in his stay when he could get no assurance from the authorities that they would be brought to Israel, he contemplated with several other Ethiopians striking against the absorption authorities. Due to the intervention of the absorption center officials, the strike never took place. He still remains uncertain as to the fate of his family and when they will join him.

His psychological state is not good, as he appears to be depressed. The subject feels that most Israelis laugh at him and are patronizing toward him. He said that although he is unemployed, he has more money in Israel than when in Ethiopia and hopes that his children can join him soon so that they can be educated in Israel. He also anticipates getting a job and having a house for his family.

The most immediate need of this olim is to locate and be reunited with his family. Until this is done, he will be unable to focus his attention on the necessary tasks for successful integration into Israeli society. The Jewish Agency and other governmental and quasigovernmental agencies working in the area of immigration should attempt to locate his family through the Israeli embassy in Addis Ababa as soon as possible. This information will allay some of the subject's anxieties and give him the opportunity to concentrate on language and vocational training, which is necessary in view of the fact that his skills are obsolete for the Israeli labor market.

The period before his family joins him may serve as beneficial if he spends it preparing for their arrival: finding adequate housing, securing a job, and making plans for the children's schooling. Crisis intervention counseling would help alleviate his extreme levels of stress, preferably counseling from an Ethiopian vatikim who has experienced similar problems himself.

Female Heads of Household

Case 1

Subject 1 is a thirty-three-year-old mother of three children ages nineteen, fifteen, and twelve. She and her children have been in Israel three months and are residing in an absorption center hotel outside of Jerusalem. The client is unemployed, having spent all of her life as a mother and housewife in Ethiopia. She has never held a job outside of the home and has no formal education or job training.

The subject came to Israel without her husband because he was incarcerated three months prior to her departure. She does not know when he will be released or if he will come to Israel afterward. Therefore she is concentrating her efforts on building a life for herself and her children in Israel alone.

The subject reports a myriad of problems since arrival such as difficulty with language and culture shock. She reports that the program at the absorption center has not helped her with these problems. She remains optimistic about her life in Israel, however, and hopes to train to become a merchant. She also hopes that her children can get a good education and fit into Israeli society. She is still undecided if her decision to immigrate was the right one for her family. "Only time can tell," she says.

This family is at risk of living on governmental assistance indefinitely if measures are not taken to prepare the mother for employment. The first step in avoiding this is to have her assessed for vocational training, while encouraging her to pursue Hebrew lessons at the ulpan. The educational needs of the children should be monitored and assistance should be given to help the mother understand the Israeli educational system, which is entirely different from that of Ethiopia. Support may also be required in terms of the discipline of children because the traditional patriarchal head of household is no longer present. Social workers can solicit the help of extended family members to assist the subject with problems surrounding child rearing in view of the absence of the father in the household.

Case 17

Subject 17 is a thirty-year-old mother of two who is a female head of household. She came to Israel with her children alone because she is divorced from their father. The subject has no formal education and has been living unemployed in an absorption center since her arrival three months ago.

She complains of the typical problems of absorption (language, culture shock, etc.). However, she also has a chronic illness. She was reluctant to reveal what the illness is, but she said since her arrival she has been quite ill and has received no medical attention nor received any medication for her condition. Quite possibly the condition is undiagnosed.

She feels extremely unhappy with her situation in Israel and is disappointed in the program at the center because it does not appear to be helping her resolve her problems. Her feelings are that, once she is finally settled in Israel, life will be very hard for her because she is the sole supporter of her family. She does exhibit feelings of optimism when discussing her children's future and hopes that they will "study hard and get a good job in Israel."

Crisis intervention is necessary for this immigrant before any long-term planning can be done for her family. An immediate evaluation of her health status should be done, tapping resources from the Ministry of Absorption so she can be seen at a hospital and referred to its social services department. Social service intervention can be initiated with her family pending the results of her medical examination.

Chapter 9

Summary: Conclusion and Recommendations

Most of the Ethiopian Jewish families in our sample were headed by males with a moderate number of children. About 20% were single parents, usually women with children. Young, single adults comprised a significant number of the vatikim interviewed. Special population groups include the aged, single parents, and female-headed households.

Ethiopian olim were generally placed in absorption centers when they first arrived in Israel; the purpose was to learn the language and find employment within a year. Due to the large number of Soviet immigrants, in combination with the emergency airlift of thousands of Ethiopians, the Jewish Agency was forced to utilize hotels and mobile homes as temporary housing.

Interviews with olim and vatikim immigrants found that most centers did not adequately address the needs of newly arrived olim, with the exception of language training at the ulpan. Learning Hebrew was identified as their most serious problem. Emotional problems were of a more urgent nature, yet there were no mental health services for these immigrants. Respondents also reported that social isolation was a problem because the centers were located on the fringe of towns and in remote parts of the country.

Despite these problems, none of the immigrants wanted to return to Ethiopia on a permanent basis, although they missed certain aspects of their lives there. Vatikim, in particular, believed that their families were better off in Israel.

Respondents held high expectations for their new lives in Israel. Jobs and education were the goals most often mentioned by respondents while, for some, living in Israel was a goal in itself. Vatikim, however, did not feel that they were reaching their goals quickly enough, and some were pessimistic about the future.

Economically, Ethiopians were at a disadvantage, as many came with nothing, having left their possessions behind in Ethiopia. Vatikim who were employed held low-paying jobs and were at the bottom of the economic scale. More serious, however, was the almost total unemployment of male heads of household in absorption centers.

The problem of unemployment was exacerbated by the presence of highly educated Soviet Jews who were forced to work at jobs far below their educational status, for these jobs could have been held by less-qualified Ethiopians. Given the high rate of unemployment in Israel (11 percent) and the continuous flow of immigrants into the country, unemployment will continue to be a serious problem for Ethiopian olim.

Racism is not a serious problem in Israel, as Ethiopians reported very little discrimination on the basis of color, although there had been some problems in regard to housing. Prejudice in the form of ethnocentrism is more problematic, as Ethiopians thought that Israelis held stereotypical ideas about them based on their African origin.

Lack of social intimacy with Israelis was common, and Ethiopians had few friends outside of their own group. Non-Ethiopian friends were often Israelis of Sephardic background or other Africans, but even those friends were few in number. Despite their lack of social interaction with Israelis, Ethiopians held favorable opinions of them, although they did not believe that Israelis felt the same toward them. Many of the vatikim thought they were perceived as "backward" and "primitive" by the public. Relationships with other immigrant groups were even more strained, most particularly with the Soviet Jews, who appear resentful of the Ethiopians' presence in Israel and are in competition with them for housing, jobs, and scarce resources.

Religion proved to be another major problem for Ethiopian Jews, as questions about their religious status continuously arose. When Ethiopians were challenged in this manner, they became insulted and reacted by demonstrating in front of government buildings. Legitimate means of airing grievances between Ethiopians and government officials did not appear to exist, so social disorder was the only way that Ethiopians could make their grievances heard.

There are many voluntary Jewish groups working to help Ethiopians overcome the initial period of adjustment in Israel. Jewish organizations and individuals showed their support by paying a bribe of $35 million for the release of Jews held in Sudan and securing their successful evacuation to Israel. The Jewish Agency has been actively involved both in Ethiopia and in Israel on behalf of Ethiopian Jewish aliya, yet the real challenge is in the future. If Ethiopians can be absorbed into Israeli society, and live in peace, and be treated with respect while keeping their identity as Jews firmly intact, then it can be said that Operations Moses and Solomon and the efforts of dedicated Jews the world over have not been wasted.

Conclusion

This book does not purport to have all the answers to the problems of the Ethiopian Jewish immigrant. In fact, it is just the beginning in a series of studies that the authors intend to conduct in the coming years with this unique population. We plan to follow them as they make new lives for themselves in Israel. It is the authors' wish, however, that the recommendations may be of some practical use to those individuals involved on a day-to-day basis with the Ethiopian immigrants and that data herein will serve as a reference point for the Ethiopian population.

We are thoroughly convinced that when the final pages of Jewish history are written, the Ethiopian Jews, whose faith and courage sustained them over centuries of exile and whose desire to return home brought them to an uncertain future in Israel, will serve as an example to those seeking religious freedom the world over.

Recommendations

Housing for Ethiopian Olim

The absorption center concept has become obsolete as a form of absorbing immigrants into the community at large and there is need for an innovative form of housing arrangement for new-comers to Israel. One of the authors of this book, Dr. Durrenda Onolemhemhen has attempted to design what is called the "Assisted Absorption Programme," which integrates the successful aspects of direct absorption with the traditional form of absorption. This would include the following components:

1. Ethiopian immigrants would be housed immediately in apartments rented by the Jewish Agency in urban and rural communities. These apartments would be scattered among private housing developments so that immigrants could live with other Israelis immediately.
2. Each Ethiopian family would be assigned a volunteer host Israeli and/or Ethiopian vatikim family who would assist the Ethiopian family with introductions, lifestyle concerns, and other settlement problems.
3. An ordinance requiring every new housing development to reserve a set number of units for immigrants should be instituted.
4. Ulpan language training would continue as usual during the initial year in Israel.
5. Periodic meetings of Ethiopian immigrants with Jewish Agency officials would be held to discuss problems encountered.
6. Vocational training would begin immediately for heads of households, with subsidized employment provided during the first two years.
7. Special programs on Israeli lifestyle, culture, and religion would be given to immigrants periodically during the first year.
8. An Ethiopian employment bureau would be established to assist employers with locating Ethiopian employees, and vice versa.
9. The Ministry of Housing would continue with its special mortgage program for Ethiopian olim.
10. Ethiopian social workers would be trained and assigned to new families to monitor their progress closely in the first year, with follow-up visits in the second and third year of immigration.
11. Meetings between vatikim and olim Ethiopian families

should be held periodically; this will fa
tion process.

12. A crisis center staffed by Ethiopian ment
sionals would be established where imn
experiencing psychosocial stress can get en
ment. A suicide prevention program is essen
13. Support groups for special Ethiopian immigra ₍e.g., single parents) would be organized.

Community Awareness

Ethnocentrism is a major barrier to the assimilation of Ethiopian Jews. This is due to the lack of awareness by Israelis of the
richness of African culture in general and Ethiopian culture in
particular. The following are recommendations to combat ethnocentrism:

1. The public and religious school curriculum should include
materials about the history of immigrant groups, such as the
Ethiopians. This should be taught from the Afrocentric perspective, most particularly in institutions where there are a
substantial number of Ethiopian pupils.
2. A public awareness campaign should be launched where ac-
curate information about Ethiopian culture is presented.
This would include film, speakers, television programs, and
radio announcements. Israeli television presently is dominated by European music and art forms.
3. Local government employees working in areas populated
by Ethiopians should attend workshops on Ethiopian beliefs, culture, and lifestyle.
4. A museum of Ethiopian Jewish history should be established in Jerusalem as a local and tourist attraction.

Religion

In the area of religion, we make the following recommendations:

1. The kessem should be reinstated as religious leaders of the
Ethiopians until adequate numbers of rabbis are trained.

2. A chief rabbi for the Ethiopians should be appointed to the Rabbinical Council.
3. Investigations regarding the authenticity of Ethiopians who are believed to be converts should be done on a case-by-case basis.

Education

In the area of education, we make the following recommendations:

1. Vocational training should be provided for heads of household in absorption centers.
2. Literacy classes should be run for all immigrants who cannot read or write. These could be incorporated into classes at the ulpans and be held in the afternoon.
3. Qualified olim (whether married or not) should be assisted with university training.
4. Priorities should be established for the training of target groups of Ethiopians for community service (doctors, nurses, school teachers, social workers, etc.).
5. Education for primary and school-age children should be directed toward academic excellence to make them competitive with Israeli children. As soon as Ethiopian children arrive, they should be placed in secular school with Israeli children and given after-school tutoring.
6. Preschoolers should be targeted for early educational programs.
7. Outreach programs involving Ethiopian parents in the education of their children should be a part of school curriculum.
8. Single mothers should be given special job training.
9. The ulpans should develop a specialized language course for elderly immigrants and Ethiopian olim with learning disabilities.

Employment

Earlier recommendations specified that Ethiopian immigrants should be given vocational training in preparation for employment in Israel and that a special bureau for the employment of Ethiopians be established. Equally important is the involvement of Ethiopian immigrants in the free enterprise system of Israel through ownership of businesses. Those businesses can in turn employ other Ethiopians and Israelis. A government policy should be established whereby:

1. Whenever possible, Ethiopian immigrants would be encouraged to utilize opportunities to establish small businesses.
2. Support in the form of training courses in business administration can be offered to immigrants.
3. Information about financial support for the establishment of small businesses through governmental and nongovernmental agencies should be made available to Ethiopian immigrants.
4. A scheme should be developed whereby government would create an incentive for the partnership of Ethiopians with other established businessmen by subsidizing the immigrant's share of the business.

Political Awareness for Ethiopian Immigrants

In a democratic country such as Israel, voting and contesting for political offices are the most common forms of citizen input in the political process. Ethiopians, as Israeli citizens, should participate actively in the decision making and policy formation processes in Israel.

To make Ethiopians politically aware, the following recommendations are provided:

1. Ethiopians should form their own political party and contest for political office at all levels of government.
2. In lieu of an independent party, a strong wing of an existing party could be established by Ethiopian citizens.
3. Voting by all eligible Ethiopians should be encouraged by sensitizing them to this process during their orientation period in Israel.
4. Ethiopians should strive to achieve key positions in the Israeli military and intelligence (Mossad).

5. Ethiopians also should strive to achieve key positions in other governmental and quasi-governmental agencies.
6. The Israeli ambassador to Ethiopia should be an Ethiopian/ Israeli Jew. This would be particularly advantageous to diplomatic relations between the two countries, as Ethiopian Israelis already would know the language, customs, and culture of Ethiopia.

Immigrant Group Relations

The relationship between Ethiopians and other immigrant groups, such as the Soviet Jews, could be improved by the following.

1. Establishing a Committee of Immigrants at the Jewish Agency to mediate disputes between immigrant groups and between the Jewish Agency and immigrants.
2. In absorption centers and caravans, immigrant committees also should be established for conflict resolution.
3. Acts of violence, racism, or discrimination on the part of immigrants against other immigrant groups should be dealt with in a timely manner by immigrant committee officials.
4. Programs should be developed around cultural diversity in settings where Ethiopians and Soviet Jews live together.

Glossary

absorption	the process of adaptation to the Israeli lifestyle
aliya(h)	the return to Israel of a Jewish population
Beta Israel	Ethiopian Jews
buda	evil eye, a person in league with evil spirits
debtera	church-educated elite
Falas Maura	Ethiopian Jews who have converted to Christianity
Falasha	an Ethiopian word meaning "strangers," the name given to the Ethiopian Jews by the dominant Amhara group in Ethiopia
Ge'ez	ecclesiastical and literary language of Ethiopia (often called **Ethiopic**)
kessem	Ethiopian Jewish priests
klitah	absorption
oleh/olim	newly arrived Jewish immigrant(s)
ulpan	Hebrew language training school
vatik/vatikim	Jewish immigrant(s) who has (have) lived in Israel for an extended period of time

Bibliography

American Association of Ethiopian Jews. 1991. *The absorption process for Ethiopian Jews: An assessment.* Washington, D.C.: AAEJ.

Ariel, Ariel, and Aycheh Seffefe. 1992. Psycholopathology among Jewish Ethiopian immigrants to Israel. *Journal of Nervous and Mental Disease* 180 (July): 465–6.

Bahrani, Z. 1990. Family and community life of Jews in Ethiopia and in the transition to Israel. In *Issues in the treatment of families from different cultures,* ed. by D. Bodovski, J. David, and Y. Eran. Jerusalem: Beithachin (Hebrew).

Bazelon, Emily. 1993. Crafting a livelihood. *Jerusalem Post* (Dec. 3): 8–10.

Ben-Barak, S. 1989. Attitudes towards work and home of Soviet immigrant women. In *The Soviet man in an open society,* ed. by T. Honwitz. Lanham, Md.: University Press of America.

Ben-David, A. 1993. Culture and gender in marital therapy with Ethiopian immigrants: A conversation in metaphors. *Contemporary Family Therapy* 5, no. 4: 327–39.

Ben-Ezer, Gadi. 1985. Cross-cultural misunderstandings: The case of Ethiopian immigrants-Jews in Israeli society. *Israel Social Science Research* 3, nos. 1–2: 63–73.

Boyd, M. 1989. Family and personal networks in international migration: Recent developments and new agendas. *International Migration Review* 23: 638–70.

Brinkley, Joel. 1991. A price for security. *The New York Times Magazine* 140 (Sept. 8): 42.

Colin, A. 1991. Medical problems of Ethiopian adolescent immigrants in Israel. *International Journal of Adolescent Medicine and Health* 3/4 (Jul.–Dec.): 271–5.

Collier's Encyclopedia, v. 9. New York: P.F. Collier, 1994: 347–61.

Coming home to a strange new land. 1991. *The Economist.* (June 1): 36.

DeVecchi, Robert P. 1994. Revise refugee policy on Haiti and Cuba. *The New York Times* (Letter to the Editor), (Jan 3): A 22.

Dinnerstein, L., R. L. Nichols, and D. M. Reimers. 1990. *Natives and strangers: blacks and indians, and immigrants in America.* London: Oxford University Press.

Dubin, Robert, and Amira Galin. 1991. Attachments to work: Russians in Israel. *Work and Occupations* 18 (May): 172–93.

Elazar, D. 1989. *The Other Jew.* New York: Basic Books.

Encyclopaedia Britannica, v. 8. Chicago: Encyclopaedia Britannica, 1968: 780–92.

Epstein, Randi Hutter. 1992. Divergent paths. *Geographical Magazine* 62 (April): 34.

Ethiopian immigrants at Galilee Mobile Home site strike to get bus stop. *The Jerusalem Post* (July 15, 1992): 12.

Ethiopian Jewry: The story of a community. 1986. Jerusalem: International Cultural Center for Youth.

Fraser, O., ed. 1991. *Operation Solomon*, Israel Al. Jerusalem: El Al Airlines.

Gerth, Jeff. 1992. U.S. can continue to return Haitian refugees, court rules. *The New York Times* 141 (Aug. 2): 10, 21.

Gergen, M. M., and K. J. Gergen. 1993. Narratives of the gendered body in popular autobiography. *The Narrative Study of Lives* 1: 191–218.

Gilad, Lisa. 1984. The transformation of the conjugal power base: Yemeni Jewish couples in an Israeli town. *Anthropologic* 26, no. 2: 191–216.

Giles, Patrick. 1993. Recent history. In *Africa South of the Sahara*, 22nd ed. London: Europa Publications: 337–340.

Gitelman, Z. 1982. *Becoming Israelis: Political resocialization of Soviet and American immigrants.* New York: Praeger.

Glenn, N. D., and K. B. Kramer. 1985. The psychological well being of adult children of divorce. *Journal of Marriage and the Family* 47: 905–12.

Glenn, N. D., and K. B. Kramer. 1987. The marriages and divorces of children of divorce. *Journal of Marriage and the Family*, 49: 811–25.

Goldberg, A. I., and A. Kirschenbaum. 1989. Black newcomers to Israel contact situation and social distance. *Sociology and Social Research: An International Journal* 74, no. 1: 52–57.

Gordon, Evelyn. 1993. Government must explain policy of settling Ethiopians. *Jerusalem Post* (Nov. 19): A 3.

Greenwood, N. 1992. *Operation Solomon: Beta Israel come home.* Israel Yearbook and Almanac 1991/1992. Jerusalem: IBRT Translation/Documentation.

Grubber, R. 1987. *Rescue: The exodus of the Ethiopian Jews.* New York: Macmillan.

Haberman, Clyde. 1993. Israel cool to admitting a new Ethiopian group. *The New York Times International* (Jan. 25): A 8.

"Haitian Refugees Center, Inc. v. Gracey," 600 F. Supp. 1396. U.S. District Court, D.C., January 10, 1985. *The American Journal of International Law* 179 (July): 744–46.

Halper, J. 1987. The absorption of Ethiopian immigrants: a return to the fifties. In *Ethiopian Jews and Israel*, ed. by M. Ashkenazi and A. Weingard. New Brunswick, N.J.: Transaction Books, 112–39.

Hanson, S. 1986. Healthy single parent families. *Family Relations* 35: 125–32.

Hetherington, E. M., M. Cox, and R. Cox. 1985. Long term effects of divorce and remarriage on the adjustment of children. *Journal of the American Academy of Child Psychiatry* 24: 518–30.

Hull, J. D. 1991. Translated in time: *Time* (June 10): 30.

Israel, Bureau of Statistics. 1991. *Immigration to Israel 1990* (unpublished report). Jerusalem.

Israeli career women guide immigrant single women. *The Jerusalem Post* (June 1991): 19.

Israel Yearbook and Almanac 1991/92, v. 46. Jerusalem: IBRT Translation/ Documentation Ltd.

Kaplan, Steve. 1992. *The Beta Israel in Ethiopia: From earliest times to the twentieth century.* New York: NYU Press.

Kessler, D. 1985. *The Falashas: the forgotten Jews of Ethiopia.* New York: Shocken Books.

Kirschten, Dick. 1993. Challenging the rules for Haitians. *National Journal* 25, no. 48: 2842.

Landau-Stanton, J. 1990. Issues and methods of treatment for families in cultural transition. In *The social and political contexts of family therapy*, ed. by M. P. Mirkin. Boston: Allyn & Bacon.

Lapidus, G. W. 1978. Women and the family: Changing attitudes and behavior. In *Women in Soviet society*, ed. by G. W. Lapidus. Berkeley: University of California Press.

Lapidus, G. W. 1988. The interaction of women's work and family roles in the USSR. *Women and Work* 3: 87–121.

Levine, Donald. 1971. The roots of Ethiopia's nationhood. In *Africa Report* (May). Washington, D.C.

Levine, Donald. 1965. *Wax and Gold.* Chicago: University of Chicago Press.

Leslau, Wolf. 1950. *Religious music of the Falashas (Jews of Ethiopia).* Princeton, N.J.: Folkways/Smithsonian, c/o Birch Tree Group Ltd.

Lewis, H. S. 1989. *After the eagles landed: The Yemenites in Israel.* London: Westview Press.

Lipsky, George A. 1962. *Ethiopia: Its people, its society, its culture.* New Haven: HRAF Press.

Lum, D. 1986. *Social work practices and people of color: A process-stage.* Monterey: Brooks/Cole.

Marras, M. R. 1980. *The politics of assimilation*. Oxford: Oxford University Press.

Marsden-Smedley, Philip. 1990. *A far country: Travels in Ethiopia*. London: Century.

Messing, S. D. 1982. *The story of the Falashas: "Black Jews" of Ethiopia*. Balshon Printing & Offset Co.

Mirsky, J., M. Barasch, and K. Goldberg. 1992. Adjustment problems among Soviet immigrants at risk. Part I: Reaching out to members of the "1000 Families" organization. *Israel Journal of Psychiatry and Related Sciences* 29, no. 3: 135–49.

Moskovitch, W. 1990. *Rising to the challenge*. London: Institute of Jewish Affairs.

Munitz, S., B. Priel, and A. Hemik. 1987. Color, skin color preferences and self-color identification among Ethiopian and Israeli-born children. In *Ethiopian Jews and Israel*, ed. by M. Ashkenazi and A. Weingard. New Brunswick, N.J.: Transaction Books.

Newman, Stanley M. 1985. Ethiopian Jewish absorption and the Israeli response: A two way process. *Israel Social Science Research* 13, nos. 1/2: 104–11.

New York Times International. 1991, 1992, 1993. New York.

Ostrovsky, V., and C. Hoy. 1990. *By way of deception: The making and unmaking of a Mossad officer*. New York: St. Martin's Press.

Parfitt, T. 1985. *Operation Moses*. London: Weidenfeld & Nicolson.

Parker, Margot. 1991. Career and employment counselling with Soviet Jewish immigrants: Issues and recommendations. *Journal of Employment Counselling* 28, no. 4: 157–66.

Quirin, James. 1992. *The evolution of the Ethiopian Jews: A history of the Beta Israel (Falasha) to 1920*. Philadelphia: University of Pennsylvania Press.

Rapaport, L. 1986. *Redemption song*. New York: Harcourt, Brace & Jovanovich.

Ratzoni, G., R. Blumensohn, A. Apter, and S. Tyano. 1991. Psychopathology and management of hospitalized suicidal Ethiopian adolescents in Israel. *Israel Journal of Medical Sciences* 27: 293–96.

Richards, L. N., and C. J. Schmiege. 1993. Problems and strengths of single-parent families: Implications for practice and policy. *Family Relations* 42: 277–85.

Rosen, Chaim. 1985. Core symbols of Ethiopian identity and their role in understanding the Beta Israel today. *Israel Social Science Research* 3, nos. 1–2: 55–62.

Rosenthal, Donna. 1992. The new exodus. *The Atlantic* 269, no. 5: 34–49.

Rudge, David. 1992. Upper Afula owners protest influx of poor immigrants. *Jerusalem Post* (July 14): 3.

Safran, C. 1987. *Secret exodus*. New York: Prentice-Hall.

Scanzoni, J., K. Polonko, J. Techman, and L. Thompson. 1989. *The sexual bond: Rethinking families and close relationships.* Newbury Park, Calif.: Sage.

Schaefer, R. T. 1993. *Racial and ethnic groups,* 5th ed. New York: Harper Collins.

Schindler, Ruben. 1993. Emigration and the Black Jews of Ethiopia: Dealing with bereavement and loss. *International Social Work* 36, no. 31: 7–19.

Schneller, Raphael. 1985. Heritage and Changes in the Nonverbal Language of Ethiopian Newcomers. *Israel Social Science Research* 3, nos. 1/2: 33–54.

Shapiro, Haim. 1994. Rabbinical courts to refrain ruling on immigrants' Jewishness. *Jerusalem Post* (May 29): A 12.

Simoons, Frederick J. 1960. *Northwest Ethiopia: Peoples and Economy.* Madison: University of Wisconsin Press.

Skinner, Elliott P. 1973. *Peoples and cultures of Africa: An anthropological reader.* Garden City, N.Y.: Published for the American Museum of Natural History by Natural History Press.

Sluzki, C. E. 1979. Migration and family conflict. *Family Process* 18: 379–390.

Sluzki, C. E. 1992. Transformations: A blueprint for narrative changes in therapy. *Family Process* 31: 217–230.

Speer, Tibbett. 1994. The newest African-Americans aren't black. *American Demographics* 16, no. 1: 9–10.

Syrkin, M. 1980. *The state of the Jews.* Washington, D.C.: New Republic Books.

Talboh, S. 1991. Few tears for the tyrant. *Time* (June 3): 36.

Ullendorff, Edward. 1960. *The Ethiopians: An introduction to country and people.* London: OUP.

Upper Afula owners protest influx of poor, immigrants. *The Jerusalem Post* (July 15, 1992): 3.

Wagaw, T. G. 1993. *For our soul: Ethiopian Jews in Israel.* Detroit: Wayne State University Press.

Waldman, M. 1985. *The Jews of Ethiopia: The Beta Israel Community.* Jerusalem: Amir-Shav, Center for Aid to Ethiopian Immigrants.

Wallerstein, J. S., and S. Blakeslee. 1989. *Second chances: Men, women, and children a decade after divorce.* New York: Ticknor & Fields.

Weingarten, M. A. 1992. *Changing health and changing culture: The Yemenite Jews in Israel.* Westport, Conn.: Praeger.

Weil, S. 1991. *Ethiopian one-parent families in Israel.* Jerusalem: Hebrew University.

Weise, Barry. *National Jewish Community Relations Advisory Council.* Unpublished paper.

Westheimer, R., and S. Kaplan. 1992. *Surviving salvation: The Ethiopian Jewish family in transition.* New York: New York University Press.

Westwood, M. J., and F. I. Ishiyama. 1991. Challenges in counselling immigrant clients: Understanding international barriers to career adjustment. *Journal of Employment Counselling* 28 (Dec.): 130–43.

Widdershoven, G. A. M. 1993. The story of life: Hermeneutic perspectives on the relationship between narrative and life history. *The Narrative Study of Lives* 1: 1–20.

Williams, C. W. 1991. *Black teenage mothers: Pregnancy and child rearing from their perspective.* Lexington, Mass.: Lexington Books.

Yonah, Y. 1991. How right wing are the Sephardim? *Tikkum* 5, no. 3: 38–102.

Zima, Suellen. 1987. Forty-two Ethiopian boys: Observations of their first year in Israel. *Social Work* 32, no. 6: 359.

Index

absorption, 45, 51, 51–91, 77–103, 105; discrimination and, 58–62; education of sample, 52–53; families of sample, 57; goals of sample, 55–57; occupations of sample, 53–54; recommendations for improving, 107–112; research on, 51–91. *See also* olim, vatikim, Ethiopian immigrants

absorption centers, 77, 79–83, 105; effects on family life, 81; stress of living in, 31; isolation of, 81; case studies of life in, 82–87; immigrants' attitudes toward, 89–91, 94–95. *See also* absorption

Agaw people, 7, 10, 18

AIDS, 64

airlifts. *See* Operation Moses, Operation Solomon, Operation Sheba, Yemenite Jews

aliya. *See* Immigration

American Association for Ethiopian Jews (AAEJ), 24

American Association of Ethiopian Jews, 35

Amhara. *See* Semitic Ethiopians

anti-Semitism, xix

Begin, Menachem, 31

Beta Israel. *See* Ethiopian Jews, Ethiopian Immigrants

buda phenomenon, 18

caravan sites, 82, 93. *See also* Housing

circumcision, 14

Cushitic Ethiopians. *See* Hamitic Ethiopians

discrimination, 58–62, 97, 106

education, 70, 72, 73, 78–79, 88, 108, 110

elderly, 88

Eritrea, 30

Ethiopia: ethnic groups, 5, 18; family, 43–48; geography, 3–4; land policy, 27; language, 5–6; religion, 6–7, 11; social life, 14; villages, 15. *See also* Haile Selassie

Ethiopian Democratic Union (EDU), 27

Ethiopian immigrants: acculturation of: *see* absorption; attitudes toward Israelis, 62; attitudes toward living in Israel, 105–

121

About the Authors

Durrenda Nash Onolemhemhen

Dr. Durrenda Nash Onolemhemhen is a native of Detroit, Michigan. She received her Ph.D. from the University of Wisconsin School of Social Work in 1979 and since that time has taught at a number of universities worldwide, including Ahmadu Bello University, Zaria, Nigeria (1979–1984). She is the author of nineteen articles in international journals and is a Rockefeller Foundation Scholar, a Fulbright Scholar, director of the Ghana International Research Training Program at Wayne State University, and coordinator of the BSW Program. She is currently associate professor at Wayne State University, School of Social Work.

Kebede Gessesse

Kebede Gessesse is a native of Ethiopia. He received his M.S. degree in library science and information from the School of Information Studies, Syracuse University, New York, in 1974 and his B.A. degree from Haile Selassie I University, Addis Ababa, Ethiopia. He is the author of several refereed journal articles in his profession. Mr. Gessesse has served in a number of teaching, management, and administrative positions worldwide, including deputy director of university libraries, Addis Ababa University, Ethiopia; documentalist, ILCA (International Organization); senior librarian/senior lecturer, University of Dar-es-Salaam, Tanzania; associate archivist, Duke Medical Center; and staff associate and library consultant for Africa News Agency, Durham, North Carolina. He has been associate professor and head of public services, Rodgers Library for Science and Engineering, University of Alabama since 1990.